Working Wood

Working Wood

A Guide for the Country Carpenter

by
Mike and Nancy Bubel

Illustrated by Liz Buell

RODALE PRESS
Emmaus PA

2   4   6   8   10   9   7   5   3

Library of Congress Cataloging in Publication Data

Bubel, Mike.
    Working wood.
    Bibliography: p.
    Includes index.
    1. Carpentry—Handbooks, manuals, etc. I. Bubel,
Nancy, joint author. II. Title.
TH5608.B8   694   77-4303
ISBN 0-87857-169-8
ISBN 0-87857-170-1 pbk.

Dedicated
to our children,
Mary Grace and Gregory,
whose
good ideas and
willingness to help
have
lightened the work
we did together.

CONTENTS

Foreword

For centuries, people have been building their own structures and devices to serve their needs. It is only in relatively recent years that we have come to expect the convenience of standardized, ready-made shelter and implements, and so have lost confidence in our own ability to design and make for ourselves the necessities of everyday life.

Mike grew up on a subsistence homestead in Poland. His family, and all the other families in his village, made or grew or bartered for just about everything they needed except shoes, salt, coffee and tea. Life was simple and work was hard in the almost-feudal Polish villages during the thirties and forties. Mike's mother wove the cloth that they used for sheets, towels and clothing. His much older brother, Vladimir, was a master carpenter who made tools, furniture, wagons and elegant horse-drawn carriages for the village landlord. Mike helped his brother in the woodshop. Since they used locally available materials and expected the product to last for years, he learned a lot about both making-do and doing things well.

Mike's early lessons in working with wood have helped us enormously in developing our own homestead. We've added to them plenty of trial and error of our own. For some years we were homesteaders at heart while living in polite, manicured neighborhoods. Then we spent four years homesteading an acre of ground down to the last inch, gradually filling in the corners of the acre with little scrap-wood shelters as our animal population grew. Now we're four years into living on the farm we'd been working toward for years. We've built a barn, equipment shed, garage, woodshed and completed many smaller projects here. Every season there is at least one new project in Mike's plan book.

The plans in this book, with the exception of the one for the tractor wagon, are his own, devised for our working homestead. They are not polished or fancy plans, but the products are sturdy and they work. In the true spirit of woodbutchery, we hope that you'll enjoy making your own adaptations of these designs for your own homestead.

Introduction

Do you save old cedar shingles and barn-door hardware? Does it pain you to see pieces of lumber, scraps of plywood, wood tables, good broom handles and sturdy apple crates, discarded as trash? Do you keep a "resource pile" behind the shed, in the barn loft or in your basement? What did you use to make the last doghouse you built—new lumber, or an old barrel, pieces of roofing and scrap siding? Would you rather look at an old barn than a new pole shed? Do some of your projects—sturdy and level though they may be—have a few honest mistakes in them? And do you find that you can live with these mistakes, as long as the thing is solid and useful? Then you're a woodbutcher too!

Don't be insulted! There are lots of us. When grandfather called a man a wood butcher, he meant that he was a poor carpenter, a bungler. That's not what we mean, though. We've taken the liberty of using the term woodbutchery in our own way. The way we see it, a woodbutcher delights in his materials, especially if he's gotten them secondhand. He is more interested in getting the job done than in what the neighbors may think of his designs. He gets an extra measure of satisfaction out of making what he needs from what he has on hand, even if he could afford to go out and buy new stuff. He has a warm feeling for his animals and likes to make them comfortable. He respects old wood. He takes pleasure in using mellow, perhaps unexpected ingredients to build what he wants. He would rather spend extra time cutting and fitting two pieces of scrap wood than to cut up a new board. He likes things to last, but doesn't mind if their shape is different.

This is no Better Homesteads and Farmsteads book. We assume that you're making a thing—a feed bin, woodshed or animal shelter—because you really need it, not because it's a good leisure time project or your neighbor has one or it would look charming right there in the front yard. As your homestead grows and develops roots and you branch out to adopt more animals, store more feed, and cut more hay and wood, you need more sheds, shelters and sturdy tools. You can make many of these things yourself, often from materials that you have on hand or can find. Very often the form of your project will grow out of the nature of what you have to work with. That is the best kind of woodbutchery; the design fits the materials at hand. That is how our garage grew—out of wood logs we had on hand and out of our need for some way of keeping the logs, and our need for shelter for our car.

Quite often, we imagine, you may be short of time, money or materials, as we were in one way or another—and sometimes in all three ways—when we accomplished some of the projects in this book. Still, you want to put up a structure that will serve your purpose, that will be safe and convenient to use, and that will stand square and sturdy so that you don't have to rebuild it next year.

The woodbutcher's way of reconciling such shortages and needs is to:

1. Keep the construction simple

2. Use found materials whenever possible

3. Consider patchwork in wood as acceptable as patchwork in yard-goods

4. Follow forms that serve the purpose, even if their shapes are un-conventional

Using found materials to fabricate homestead structures may be rooted in necessity, but often the object that grows from your labors has a special quality of appropriateness to your homestead, so that in the end you'd never trade it for a slick store-bought gizmo or prefab.

The project plans that we detail in this book are meant not to be followed absolutely, but to be adapted to your situation. These structures that we've worked out constitute our response to the requirements of our homestead critters and tasks. Rather than follow these plans down to the inch, though, let them suggest to you what you can do on *your* place, with what *you* have on hand. In many cases, the measurements of a given piece that we've made were dictated by the number of boards that we had in usable condition in a certain length, as in our equipment shed—or the space into which something would fit, as in our feed bins. As long as you keep your changes in scale with the design as a whole, you shouldn't run into any trouble. There's no reason, for example, why you couldn't build the mangers longer, the feed bin wider, the garage taller.

Working on these embellishments to our homestead—puzzling over the design, scaring up the materials, struggling, sometimes, to get the things built and now using them with much satisfaction—has put us in touch with ourselves, helped us to trust our instincts about what we really need after all, and given us an inkling of what we can accomplish when we work together. We wish the same for you, fellow wood-butchers!

PART I

Chapter One

Sources of Wood and Other
Building Materials

For many woodbutchers, purchasing wood is a last resort. We have had to buy new wood occasionally, when we needed rafters, for example, but we would far rather use good old wood from a wrecked building. And not only to save money, either. Certainly, we save money—and we don't mind that a bit—but we also get 2 by 4s and 6 by 10s that really measure 2 by 4 and 6 by 10 (unless the torn-down building was built quite recently). As you probably know, lumber sold today as 2 by 4s and 6 by 10s or whatever, actually measures less. (Last we heard, you still get full measure on length, though!)

You can also get all kinds of useful extras like storm windows, doors, concrete blocks, hardware, interesting iron grillwork, stained glass windows, fireplace mantels, shutters, electrical conduits, thermostats and sheet metal when you salvage wood. You may find some choice weathered siding—the kind commercial panelling strives so hard to imitate. This stuff all comes as a hodgepodge, of course, some of it "as is"—none of it neatly stacked and arranged—but we've found it worthwhile to keep a good stock of these extras with their great potential. We've often found uses for them within a few years. It's handy to have a shed or barn loft to store these things in, to keep the farm from looking like a junk-and-used-parts shop.

Jerry Belanger, writing in *Countryside* magazine some time ago, mentioned that few homesteaders have a chance to breathe the heady aroma of new-wood sawdust; the dust from cutting the old wood that many of us like to use is less pungent. There's another thing about using recycled wood: it requires much more cutting and fitting, patching and customizing than new wood, since the lengths available to you are seldom standard or uniform. You must often cut around a weak spot or try to salvage an almost-long-enough board that was splintered in being removed from its building. Making things with used wood sometimes takes a little more time than building with new lumber. In fitting on our barn siding, for example, we had to measure and cut each piece of the tongue-and-groove siding individually, searching for just the right board for a given spot: not too long—we'd need the long ones to go up to the roof peak—but not too short, because the groove on the neighboring piece was chipped in several places. Building with old wood can get to be a treasure hunt, especially if you try as we do not to cut into a long piece if there's a short one around that will do the job. You can spend a lot of time finding and assembling your "candidates."

We don't by any means intend to imply that used wood is the only appropriate material for woodbutchery. Apart from the fact that we don't enjoy buying it, we have nothing against new wood. We like all kinds of wood. But you know where to find new lumber—either at the lumberyard or, if you're lucky, in your own woodlot (assuming you have access to a sawmill). The good used stuff takes a little more looking.

Once you start to hunt up sources of used wood around your town and countryside, you may well be surprised—as we were—to find out how many perfectly good buildings are being junked. There are all sorts of reasons for this. In a town near us, for example, a solid old brick schoolhouse must be replaced because it doesn't meet fire code regulations. New roads being built may displace houses, garages and barns that might be sources of good sound wood. Zoning changes, as towns expand, sometimes necessitate the wrecking of barns and chicken houses.

Parking lots and shopping centers, in their lamentable asphalt spread, often uproot usable buildings. Obsolete wood silos, yielding long tongue-and-groove boards without nails, are sometimes just left to rot. We've seen a fine old carriage house taken down when a bank needed more parking space, a chicken house razed and burned when the business became unprofitable, a two-story home dismantled to make room for a shopping mall and an old barn on the edge of a small city become

a burden to the businessman on whose commercial property it stood—
a bonanza to the young couple who took it down, numbered every
piece, and reconstructed it on their farm.

Other sources of raw materials for making homestead necessities
include the following:

• Newspaper publishers often sell the thin aluminum plates used in
printing the paper for 10¢ or 25¢ each. These plates may be folded in
half for use as shingles, cut to form stovepipe collars, nailed on grain
bins to keep out rodents, or tacked to chicken house walls to keep out
drafts.

• Dumps are great community resources where you may find steel cable,
storm windows, wood cable spools, scrap wood, pieces of metal roofing,
and who knows what else. Once we found a 7-foot length of brand-new

Formica countertop surface. If we had more trash to take to the dump, we'd probably have a chance at many more usable finds.

• Dealers in snowmobiles, gravestones and other heavy goods that need protection in transit often have wood crates, usually dismembered, that they must pay a trash man to haul away. The businessmen we have dealt with have been glad to have us remove as many discarded crates as we could use.

• Railroad and telephone companies sometimes sell used railroad ties and telephone poles.

You can always buy your lumber, of course. If you do, be sure to inspect what you're getting and avoid purchasing boards that are warped

the local Sawyer

or that have many knots. This is, admittedly, easier to do when buying small quantities of boards.

Another way to get the building materials you need is to cut standing timber on your own place and have it cut into boards at a sawmill. Rural sawmill owners seldom advertise. The work is often a sideline and you might be pleasantly surprised, as we were, to discover that there is a working sawmill—small but adequate—in your neighborhood. Ask around and make your arrangements before cutting your trees.

When we built our barn here on the farm, we used recycled wood for every bit of it. Our wood came from two sources:

1. A large old 100-by-20-foot asbestos-lined, two-story brooder house, purchased for $135 from a retirement home. It was out of place on their grounds, and they had already started taking it down. This long, sturdy building was a source of excellent rafters, siding, posts and planks—plus a lot of miscellaneous wiring, wood cages, feeders, windows and aged chicken manure.

2. A lovely old barn, well-roofed, with heavy timbers, oak plank flooring and sturdy sills that was smack in the path of a sewage line, right next to a busy road. It had to come down, and we were only too glad to agree to get it down in time to spare its owner a fine.

In both cases, we paid a man to wreck the building for us since we were busy setting up our homestead. Even at that, we got a pile of good lumber worth many times its cost to us. Those who do their own wrecking save even more. You're probably wondering whether there are any good old buildings left out there for you to salvage. We wouldn't tantalize you with this news of our good fortune if our experience was just an isolated bit of good luck. On the contrary, sound, sturdy buildings are abandoned or taken down, somewhere, in most every county. Now we can't give any guarantees, naturally, but we'd be very surprised if you couldn't turn up at least one reusable building after a few weeks of serious looking. To conduct a systematic search for buildings to be wrecked in your area, we'd suggest you do the following:

1. *Look.* Sometimes by driving around, you can spot clues that tell you that a building must be taken down: sewer pipes stacked by the road,

a "for sale" sign on a farm next to an apartment complex, an empty chicken house, a sign declaring that a new building will be erected on a certain site, demolition already in progress, a boarded-up house. Follow it up, then, find the owner of the building or the town councilman who can tell you what will be happening there.

If you can catch these clues of change and investigate them while the owner is still wondering what to do with the unwanted building, you stand a good chance of arriving at a deal that helps both of you. He saves money and trouble. You get lumber and often windows, bricks, doors, fixtures and interesting trivia.

2. *Ask.* The real centers of action and contact in a rural area are often the feed store, the lumberyard, the hardware store, the locally owned grocery store. Tell the good people in these shops what you're looking for. They generally have an ear to the ground and might know or hear something that would give you a valuable lead. We've found, in trying to track down items we need in our rural community, that you can start almost anywhere to ask. Perhaps the first person we call isn't able to give us the information we need, but he knows someone who might, and often after five phone calls and many interesting conversations we've found the butcher or hog raiser or sheep shearer we were looking for. Contacts lead to other contacts. Get in touch.

3. *Read.* Watch the newspaper, especially the local community weekly, which can give you leads of two kinds:

a. Classified ads. We've seen a good many ads in small town papers offering buildings to be wrecked. Some of the buildings were even free for the taking.

b. Straight news. Look for the implications of news announcements. An old movie house is to be torn down. A small factory in town on a street of row homes is expanding. A farm is being divided into lots. A new shopping center is planned. A citizens' group is protesting town plans to raze a historic building. (But perhaps you should join *them!*) Wrecking of such places as old ballrooms or schools is often featured in weekly papers as a straight news item. An old house in Indiana that was once ours had warmly beautiful maple floors that had been transplanted from an old ballroom. Wood lives on!

Read, also, the community bulletin boards that are often posted in grocery and feed stores.

4. *Advertise.* Make your wants known by placing a classified ad, posting a notice on public bulletin boards, even hanging a sign on your mailbox.

Change is constant, it seems, in new communities and old. If you can find out what's changing in your area, you'll most likely be on the trail of some good used wood.

It's entirely possible that an intensive search may turn up more than one building that must be dismantled. You may even have a choice. In that case, you'll want to evaluate each building carefully, in terms of its condition, the probable ease of wrecking, and how much it has of the kind of wood you need most. Important areas to check are:

- size and soundness of rafters, beams, posts, framing 2 by 4s and 3 by 6s, siding
- condition of roof
- size and kind of doors and windows
- possible useful extras such as bricks, fences, concrete blocks, electrical wiring, stairs, shutters
- proximity to other buildings that might make safe dismantling difficult

Look for evidence of termite damage and dry rot. A building with a caved-in or partly absent roof may have wood too rotten to bother with.

If the building is a house and there are usable extras like old furniture or hardware left around, be sure to get clear specifications from the owner as to whether these findings are to go with the building or to be set aside for him. Let the owner know when work will be started so that he or she can remove any wanted articles before then. Houses, with their plaster, wire and plumbing often take more time to wreck than barns, sheds or garages.

If you take down a house, save the plaster for your compost heap rather than carting it to the dump. Plaster from an old wall we took out of one of our houses had horsehair embedded in it. All the better for the garden!

We strongly recommend taking a written inventory of the building you will salvage, recording the number of windows and doors; approximate number and sizes of rafters, beams, posts, and planks, furring strips, framing lumber; approximate square footage of siding; area of roof; and any extras like plumbing or loose building supplies that go with the building. This will both help you to plan your new building projects and give you a checksheet to keep track of what you actually do receive from the building.

In planning most of our homestead buildings, the dimensions were determined by the sizes of lumber that we had available.

Even if you have no immediate use for the lumber, you'd no doubt be wise to get hold of a good give-away building when it's available, if you can work out a way to store the wood.

Chapter Two

Salvaging Old Buildings

Once you find a source of wood—a building that, for one reason or another, must be razed—you have a new problem. Or a decision, at any rate. Will you take the building down yourself, or will you hire someone to wreck it for you? The obvious trade-off here is money for time, and perhaps also for skill, for there is a knack to taking down a building safely and with the least damage to the wood. We elected to hire the job done since we were a little more short of time than we were of money.

For our first building, the brooder house, we hired a man who made his living wrecking buildings. How did we find him? We read his ad offering a dismantled carriage house for sale. When we called him, we found that, although that advertised building had already been sold, he had rights to several more salvageable buildings and also did custom wrecking. To find such a person in your area, you might check the yellow pages, advertise, or ask at the hardware store or local junk-and-used-parts shop. They'll probably be acquainted with him. The dumpmaster will also be likely to know him, since a man in the wrecking business must often get a special permit to dump unusable scrap. Try the people at the bank, too; they know what's going on in town.

The man who took down the brooder house for us agreed to truck the parts from the wrecking site near our former homestead to our new home on the farm, in another county.

When, later in the summer, we found a barn that could be had free for the taking, we were more pressed for time than ever. We had started constructing our new barn, but we needed more wood and we also needed to make every day count so that we could get the barn sided and roofed over before the end of summer vacation for Mike and the children. This time we made a different arrangement. A neighbor offered to take the old barn down and truck the wood to us for a cash payment of $150 and the almost-new aluminum roof, which he needed for a concrete block barn he was building. This suited both families very well, and although the neighbor was not an experienced wrecker, he had razed a barn before. His method was unorthodox, but it was effective: He and his helper removed the roof and siding, knocked out some of the framing pins, and collapsed the structure by pulling it down with a heavy-duty tractor linked to an upper beam by a steel cable. The thud of the falling building was horrendous, but there was surprisingly little damage to the framing members. Either he knew what he was doing, or he was lucky.

If you intend to salvage a building yourself, may we offer a few words of advice.

Dismantling the old barn has begun. *Mike Bubel*

The wood will be used in our barn.

Mike Bubel

Equipment at hand

1. If at all possible, find a helper or two to work with you. It's safer and easier than working alone.

2. You'll need the following equipment:
   - crowbars—one for each person and then some.
     They're not expensive.
   - hardhats—for large buildings
   - hammers
   - heavy rope
   - liquid wrench
   - screwdrivers
   - nail-pulling pinchers
   - "Wunderbar" prying bar

- saws—carpenter's, bow saw and/or chain saw
- hacksaw for cutting metal
- pliers
- extension ladder
- use of a large truck—flatbed or dump

Optional:
- pulley or "come-along"
- 8-pound mallet
- wedges
- safety shoes
- steel cable and tractor—for pulling building down

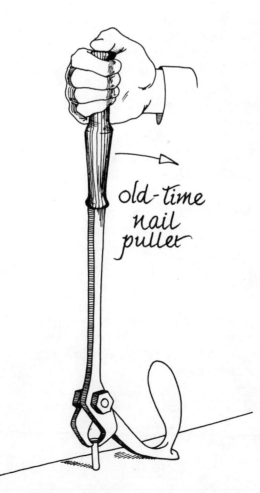

old-time
nail
puller

3. Study the building before tackling it. How was it put together? Where was it pinned? Toenailed? How is it braced?

4. Take out doors and windows first to remove hazard of breakable glass.

5. Remove the "skin" of the building next—the siding, barn doors, ventilator louvres and the roof—before starting on the framing.

6. If you want to save old beams with their corner joinery intact, carefully knock out the pins and lower the beams individually, using a pulley and a heavy rope.

7. If possible, truck away each day's salvage to reduce accident-causing clutter at the site and to discourage vandalism, as well as to facilitate gradual piling of the goods at their destination.

8. Leave the site as clean as possible after wrecking the building. Litter breeds litter.

9. Remember that the structure weakens as you remove parts of it. If in doubt, take no chances on the stability of a wall or beam.

10. Loosen barn siding by banging on it from the inside of the building—much quicker than prying it off from outside.

11. Always check to be sure that electric power has been disconnected before tackling a wired building.

12. Leave splintered or rotten ends on otherwise good boards, rather than neatly trimming them off. They can be cut to your exact specifications later. We have occasionally chopped off a board end that we later wished we had left on.

13. Use special care in salvaging tongue-and-groove boards, to save the tongue-and-groove intact, as much as possible. You'll be glad you did, later, when you want to join them again!

In addition to your own safety and that of your helper, you need to take steps to forestall possible harm to others not directly involved in your wrecking project. For example:

1. Some old buildings are unsafe to begin with, and when weakened in the gradual process of wrecking, they may be a hazard to neighborhood children who are tempted to play on them or in them. As soon as you know that an old building is yours, whether by purchase or agreement, post a NO TRESPASSING sign on all four sides of it.

2. Warn neighbors in plenty of time to remove children and pets, and also cars, from within range of a building that is to be collapsed.

3. If a building to be razed is very close to a street, as our barn was, alert the local traffic police and be sure to have a flagman ready to stop

Posting Signs for Safety

17

cars when the building is to be pulled down. You know generally in which direction the building will fall, but you can't predict where flying parts might land.

In some cases, you must sign a contract agreeing to complete demolition of a building by a certain date. If you are taking down the building yourself, you can be reasonably sure whether you will be able to complete the project in the required time. If someone else is doing the job for you, you might be wise to set up a contract with him so that he agrees to have the building removed by a certain definite time.

When we bought the brooder house (and we found later that the authorities were very anxious to get rid of it and probably would have given it to us) we had to sign an agreement to have the building removed by a certain time. Our wrecking expert also worked by contract. We agreed to pay him part of his fee before he started the work, with the remainder due on completion. We added a clause to the contract stipulating that the building should be taken down by the date required in our contract with the owners of the building.

The arrangements we made for the barn were much less formal. We gave the barn owners a $25 deposit to hold the barn for us until we could find someone to dismember it. (We were so glad for the good wood in the barn and so grateful to the owners, who later turned down a chance to sell the barn because they'd made an agreement with us, that we felt the least we could do would be to let them keep our deposit.) Our agreement with our neighbor was by handshake. He did his part and we tried to do ours.

Chapter Three

Storing Your Wood

A stockpile of good usable wood is a valuable homestead resource. You've spent time or money, maybe both, to get it, whether you bought new wood, cut and sawed seasoned lumber from your own woodlot, or salvaged an old building. Your stockpile is full of potential. In order to get full value from your wood, you will want to keep it in good condition.

Poorly stored wood soon spoils. When wood is in contact with the ground or piled with one board resting directly on top of another, it remains damp and may rot within a year. Long boards tossed into a helter-skelter pile may warp and twist along the long axis. Even solid beams and planks can start disintegrating back into the earth in a surprisingly short time if they cannot dry out on all sides after rain. If you see mold begin to grow on your stored wood, it needs more air circulation.

Now you can't bring all that wood into the house with you, we realize that. Wood is amazingly durable, even when left in the rain, as long as it has a chance to dry promptly after becoming wet.

Lumberyards keep some wood under open-sided sheds. If you have some good lumber that you won't be using for a few years, you might want to put up a simple four-pole shed with open sides and sloping roof to protect your good lumber from the worst of the weather. You can always store firewood in the shed after it's served its primary purpose, or dismantle it and add the parts to your stockpile.

Not many of us, though, begin with enough wood or time to spare that we can stop to erect a lumber-protecting shed. We're anxious to get on with the business of building up a homestead. You can store well-stacked wood out in the open for as long as five years, sometimes longer, depending on your climate, without significant loss. We have piles of wood here on the farm that have been stored for four years. The wood is still in good condition.

Suppose you have a big pile of assorted lumber just delivered to your place by your friendly neighborhood house wrecker, as we did during our first months here on the farm. The goat kids think you've put it there just for them to climb on and the sheep appreciate the shade cast by the pile and crop the grass around the edges. You know, though, that you've got to do *something* about that wood or it'll spoil. But where do you begin?

Sort the lumber first, at least roughly, so that you know what you have. You might designate separate piles for 2 by 4s, 3 by 6s, 2 by 10s, 4-by-4 posts, heavy oak planks, 1-by-2-inch furring strips, notched rafters, doors, and such. As you sort, set aside a collection of approximately 1-inch thick by 12-inch long pieces: split sticks of siding, lath, scrap wood and the like, that won't be good for building. Those are your spacers to keep air circulating in your woodpile.

Choose a site for your stockpiles. You want to keep them off of low ground where water might collect, in places that are accessible to your tractor or cart, yet not so close to the house that you'll consider them an eyesore when they're still around in two years. If you're in copperhead country, keep your piles well away from the house.

If possible, orient your woodpiles with the cut ends facing your prevailing winds; when rain blows into the pile, less wood will be soaked, since the rain won't strike such a large area. The open-pored wood ends will dry sooner.

More important, elevate the first layer of wood 8 to 10 inches above ground level. We think it is worth buying cement blocks for this purpose. They won't rot and can always be used around the homestead when you use up the woodpile. Sometimes you can find second-hand cement blocks and these, of course, work just fine.

We've made lumber piles with just a 3-to-4-inch log separating the bottom layer from the ground, but we've found that the more

Working at the lumber pile.   *Nancy Bubel*

generous 8-to-10-inch spacing preserves the wood better. More air circulates underneath the pile and animal nests are less likely to pile up and contact the wood. Cats can get underneath, too, to keep down nesting rodents.

We always put the worst wood on the bottom of the pile, and that most likely to be used soon on the top. (Sometimes we guess wrong!) Leave about a half-inch space between boards in a pile. If the pieces of wood in certain pile are all the same size, leave the same amount of space between them throughout the pile so that there is good drainage of rain all the way down.

If the stockpiles of wood contain too many different sizes and kinds of lumber, lots of time is wasted in taking the pile apart when you need wood. And, around here at least, there's not always time to put the pile together well.

Before putting a second layer of wood on the pile, arrange spacers of lath or scraps approximately 1 by 1 or 1 by 2 inches across the wood. These spacers insure air circulation so the wood can dry after a rain. Without them the pile of wood will soon rot.

Storing lumber

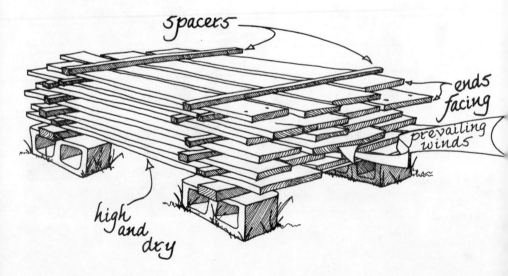

spacers

ends facing

prevailing winds

high and dry

The spacers should be sturdy, but as narrow as possible. The smaller the area of contact with the stored wood, the better. In one pile of siding that we stacked, using only a 3-to-4-inch spacing above the ground, we placed spacers of 3-inch tongue-and-groove siding. That was too wide. The 1-inch boards rotted out where the wide siding touched them and prevented them from from air drying.

Long pieces of lumber should be supported by spacers in the middle as well as at the ends, to prevent sagging. Two by 4s should be

T. L. Gettings

Hay stacked on a platform supported by concrete blocks. These excellent oak planks make a sturdy, convenient hay platform in the barn, easily taken apart if we should need the planks for another building.

supported by a spacer every 4 to 6 feet. Heavy beams can get by with 10-to-12-foot spacing.

Another thing: if some beams and posts have troughs or depressions in them that might catch and hold rain—as some of ours did from old peg holes and carpenter's gouges—be sure that these water-catching sides of the lumber are face down, not up, as you stack them in the pile.

When a pile will be in place for some time, we sometimes protect it further by topping it with old planks, sections of roofing, rubber sheets or other homestead findings to shed rain.

We've found it possible to store some exceptionally sound or attractively grained boards under roof by using them for:

1. Loose planking in barn and garage loft. Planks also may be piled in the loft under the eaves where they won't take up valuable floor space.

2. Hay platform in the barn: our way of "storing" some excellent 2-by-12-inch oak planks. Set on 3 by 6s supported by concrete blocks, they keep the hay up off the floor so that mice and rats don't nest under it. And they are ready at any time for any other more urgent purpose we might have for them.

3. Canning shelves, made of double 2 by 10s separated by cement blocks. These are mighty stout shelves, but we had the wood so it didn't make sense to buy any newer, flimsier boards. Here again, if and when we need these planks, they are easily accessible. Meanwhile, they serve a useful purpose.

4. "Temporary" bookshelves in an extra room, made of barn siding spaced by stacks of old books.

Your stockpile has in it the beginnings of all those bins, sheds and shelters that you need on your homestead. The time necessary to stack it carefully and protect it is well spent.

Chapter Four

Removing Nails and Findings

Old lumber often comes with an interesting assortment of hardware—old latches, hand-forged hooks and foot-long strap hinges, many of which are sought by antique collectors. We like these old pieces that evoke thoughts of all the farmers through the years who have thumbed the latches on the old barn on their way in to care for their stock. Rather than mount them for display, though, we prefer to use them, and so we build old hinges, hooks and latches into our new buildings. That way we can enjoy them every day.

Nails in used lumber can be a problem or a resource depending on how much time you have, or can take. You may feel that really old cut nails are worth saving as an example of another way of doing things. Old nails can be reused. It doesn't matter if they are dull, as long as they're sturdy and straight. To straighten a used nail, place it on the crosscut surface (cut across the grain, not with the grain) of a log or block of wood, and bang it with a hammer.

We gave our children, Mary Grace and Gregory, the job of removing nails from our used lumber, paying them by the pound for what they extracted. At times, we all worked together at the job, when we urgently needed a certain kind of lumber from the pile. One day in particular stands out in memory: we spent the morning on the hillside above the house, removing nails from boards. The sky was the kind of cloudless blue usually seen on calendar pictures and the air was still cool. Below us at the edge of the meadow, the barn foundation lay

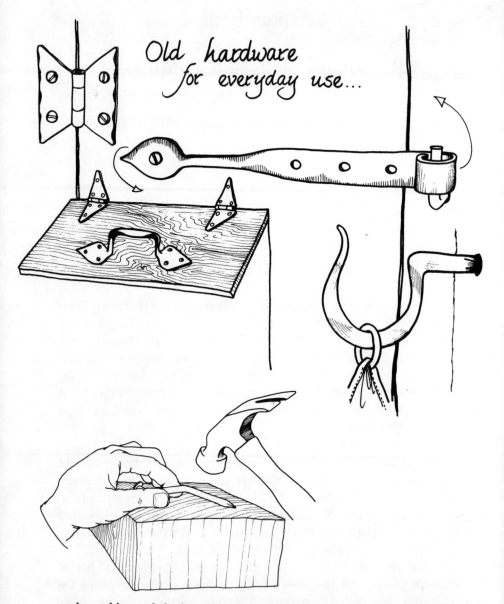

Old hardware
for everyday use...

ready, and beyond the barn in the hayfield our neighbor was cutting our hay, his share and ours. The trees surrounding the hayfield blended into the hills beyond. The bees were working the blackberry blossoms. As we kept reminding each other between taking deep breaths of that winey air now fragrant with hay, if we hadn't had the nails to work on we might easily have missed the whole scene.

If you don't have time to remove the nails from your wood before stacking it, you can pile the boards parallel at random and leave the nails in; they will help to space the wood so that air can circulate.

Even the job of nail removal has its fine points. Perhaps some of the pointers we picked up in dealing with our nail-studded wood treasure will help to save your thumbs or your temper if you find yourself with a pile of boards bristling with nails.

First, be warned that you can ruin a good claw hammer by using

Mike Bubel

To straighten a screw or threaded bolt, use a small block of wood as a buffer so that the threads will not be flattened by the hammer.

27

it to remove large or rusty nails and to pry boards apart. Roofing tacks won't hurt the hammer, if you can get its edge under the nail head, but otherwise use a crowbar for all nail removal. The "Wunderbar," a 2-inch-wide instrument with one end notched and hooked and the other tapered to a thin edge, is an invaluable tool for removing nails. If a nail is embedded so that you cannot fit the crowbar tip under its head, use a hammer or rubber mallet to bang the tapered edge of the "Wunderbar" under the nail head. You can then raise the head enough to give the crowbar purchase on it.

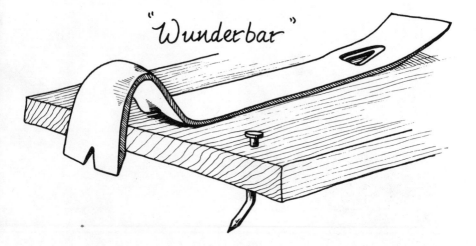

If you have a board with nails embedded up to their heads but sticking out on the underside, bang them from the pointed end back through the wood, just enough to admit the crowbar. If you bang them too far through, it is more difficult to get leverage to remove them.

When a large nail protrudes several inches from the wood, put a small block of wood under your crowbar to give it better leverage.

Always have a widemouthed container like an old pail or paint bucket handy to collect the nails you are removing, so that they don't get scattered on the ground. Bent old nails can do expensive damage to tractor tires. Also, if you use scrap ends of wood containing nails for firewood, keep the ashes from that wood separate for spreading around trees or other noncultivated areas. Nails don't do anything for Roto-tiller blades, either.

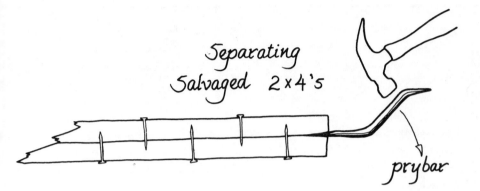

Separating
Salvaged 2 x 4's

prybar

Prying two nailed boards
apart

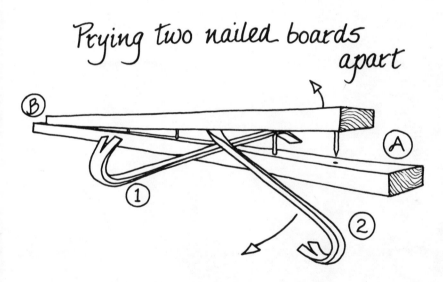

Ⓑ

Ⓐ

①

②

Crowbar ① is used
as a fulcrum for crowbar ②
to pry boards apart.
Crowbar ① also keeps boards separate
while working toward end Ⓑ from end Ⓐ

If nails are rusted in the wood and they break off when you try to pull them out, loosen the rust first by driving the nail *into* the wood a short distance. Then pull it out. If a screw is "frozen" by rust, hit it with a hammer to loosen it.

Sometimes you need a rust solvent and much patience to remove the screws from old hinges; often the threads are rusted away and the screw simply revolves when turned with a screwdriver. It is sometimes necessary to loosen a screw and then to remove it with a nail puller. If a hinge is too rusted to open and close easily, brush on rust solvent and use a hammer to bang the hinge open and closed, back and forth on a wood block so that the solvent will penetrate the cracks between the parts. Most of the hinges we treated in this way limbered up enough to use.

If you lose a nail head while working on it, you will be glad for a pair of nail-pulling pinchers to help you complete the job of removing the nail. These are also useful for removing staples. Another way to

Mike Bubel

Using nail-removing pliers to pry headless nails out of furring strips.

deal with headless nails is to drive them on through the wood with a punch or another nail.

Straighten bent nails that won't pull through by holding a crowbar up next to them and banging them with a hammer.

We salvaged many good 2 by 4s that were nailed together from both sides by using the following procedure:

1. Drive thin-edged crowbar, wedge or "Wunderbar" into the crack between the boards, at the end. Pry them apart as much as possible.

2. Put a wedge or another crowbar in the small opening between the boards.

3. Use that crowbar as a fulcrum to pry the boards open still further with your other crowbar.

4. Work your way down the length of the boards like this until they are completely pried apart.

Chapter Five

The Art of Persuasion

Techniques of moving and positioning heavy wood

Should your source of recycled wood be an old barn or even a house with sturdy joists and sills, you'll find yourself the new owner of some massive pieces of lumber. (And, incidentally, with a new respect for the barn builders of old!) The old barn that we had taken down yielded a treasure of sound 100-year-old framing beams, posts and planks, in sizes ranging from 10-by-12-inch beams 30 feet long down to 1-inch furring strips.

These large, heavy lengths of oak, pine and fir lumber were splendid potential building material, but far too heavy for two people to lift. Many weighed about 600 pounds and a few were an estimated 1,000 pounds. How would we ever position them in a storage pile, much less raise them into place in a building?

Like many other homesteaders, we have found the truth of farm-oriented homilies coming home to us with new clarity. We learned a new appreciation of "make hay while the sun shines" in our hay field. And, faced with a stack of marvelously sturdy but fiendishly heavy wood, we began to experience the reality of the maxim: "where there's a will, there's a way." We certainly wanted to use that wood. And so we gradually worked out a system of sorts that made it possible to get a giant beam from one place to another without wrecking our backs.

The methods we used to move heavy pieces of wood were simple and basic—applied high school physics, really—and anything but original; people have been coaxing heavy objects around for centuries using these methods of persuasion.

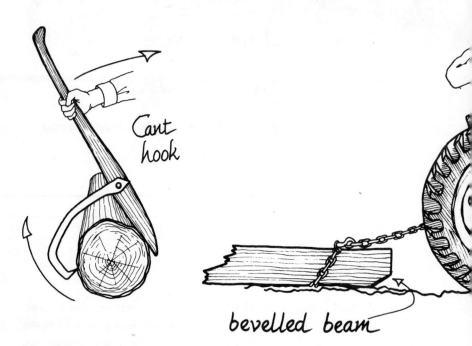

Cant hook

bevelled beam

ROLL IT: When a heavy log must be moved a short distance, rolling it is often the simplest way to do the job. Use a cant hook or the curved end of a crowbar to roll very large pieces of wood. At the same time, one or two people on the other side of the log can push to begin the roll. Watch out for your toes!

SLIDE IT: For short distances, have two people each hook a crowbar on the log and pull. You can move more weight by sliding than you can lift. We moved many impossibly heavy pieces of wood long distances by linking a chain around the end of the lumber and pulling it with our tractor, sliding it directly on the ground. To prevent the sharp forward end of the beam from gouging the soil, you can cut a bevel in it.

USE A RAMP: To get our heavies up onto the storage pile, we improvised a ramp, using 2-by-4 and 4-by-6-inch lumber. We rolled the lumber up the ramp and over onto the pile. Our largest pieces, the rough 10-by-12 lumber that had supported the floor of the barn where the tractor was parked, required some extra persuasion. We enlisted the help of visiting friends and with six of us rolling the wood it went up easily with no strain at all.

...or a
shortened chain
to lift and drag

improvised ramp

POLE TRANSPORT: We had some long 2-by-12-inch oak planks that were too heavy for two people to lift. Four of us could manage them, though, when we slid two sturdy poles or short 1 by 4s under the plank—one on each end, leaving enough pole on each side for a hand-hold. With each of us holding one end of a pole, we had the effectiveness of a double team and were able to put these beautiful old planks where we wanted them. When carrying any heavy object as a team, whether two or four people, remember to keep in step, or you'll be working against each other and making the job harder than necessary.

keeping in step.......

LEVERING: When it comes to getting heavy wood to go where you want it, you can't beat the old back-saving method of levering. For levers, we used crowbars, 2 by 4s or 3-inch cedar poles. (A length of hornbeam, also called ironwood—an understory tree that seldom grows to a large diameter—makes an excellent lever. The wood is hard and endures a large amount of strain). To give our levers power, we used a fulcrum, a log or concrete block point of support, on which the lever pivoted when lifting the load.

When you have a heavy weight to lift, you want to get maximum lift power from minimum exertion. Using your effort in the most efficient way can sometimes make an overwhelming job possible. One of our "trade secrets" that has helped us to persuade heavy stuff to go where we wanted it is an understanding (Mike's understanding, that is!) of one of the force principles of mechanics.

Don't panic. We're not going to get ultra-technical on you. Here's an example that illustrates what we're talking about:

Suppose you have a heavy 12-foot beam to be carried by two people. If the beam is fairly uniform along its entire length, the same amount of force will be needed to raise one end of it, as to raise the other. When the two people handling the beam stand at the extreme ends of it, each person bears an equal weight.

But suppose that the person stationed at one end of the log decides to move his support of the wood from the extreme end to a point one-fourth of the way toward the center of the log, or to put it another way, to a point halfway between the end of the log and the log's center of

Nancy Bubel

Rolling a heavy log up a ramp with the help of friends.

gravity in the middle. That person then assumes a load twice as heavy as his partner is carrying at the extreme end of the log.*

For example if the beam weighs 180 pounds, then each person supporting an end of the beam carries 90 pounds. But if Nancy supports the log at the extreme end, and Mike holds it at a point halfway between his end and the middle of the log (the center of gravity in a uniform log), then Mike is carrying 120 pounds and Nancy only 60. Got that?

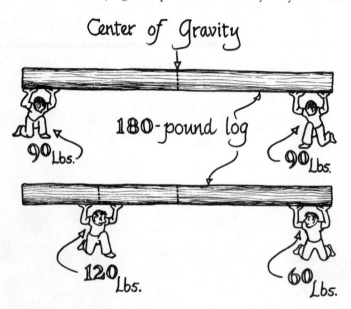

*Diagram of the beam with the forces acting on it:

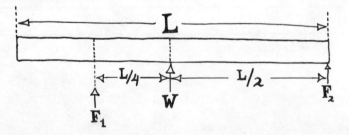

From the equilibrium condition of the forces acting on the log, expressed as an equation: $F_1L/4 = F_2L/2$, from which we derive that $F_1 = 2F_2$. L represents the length of the log. F_1, in this case, is the force exerted by the person positioned at a point one-fourth of the way from one end of the log—this is, at a distance L/4 from the center of gravity. F_2 represents the force exerted by the other person, positioned at the distance L/2 from the center of gravity, at the extreme end of the log. W is the weight of the beam acting at the point of the center of gravity.

By moving in one-fourth of the distance on the beam toward the center of gravity, Mike has assumed twice the load that Nancy carries. Moral: unless you're trying to equalize uneven strength in a team, always carry your load at the end.

This same principle governs your use of a lever, too. Let's say that you are balancing your crowbar on a fulcrum to raise the end of a beam from the ground. Since the other end of the beam rests on the ground, you need raise only one-half its weight. The ground supports the other half. Okay. If the beam weighs 1,000 pounds, that's 500 pounds you must lift.

500 pounds to be lifted by crowbar

$^{5/6}$ **F_2**

$^{1/6}$

1,000-pound beam

ground supports 500 pounds

F_1

fulcrum placed for maximum efficiency

If you arrange a fulcrum with one-sixth of the crowbar length extending from the fulcrum to the beam, and five-sixths protruding between the fulcrum and you, then only 100 pounds of force will be needed to lift one end of a 1,000-pound log.*

When the fulcrum is moved to a point one-fourth of the way in from the weight-bearing tip of the crowbar, you must exert one-third of the total weight to be lifted (500 pounds), or 166 plus pounds, to raise the end.

* $F_2 = \dfrac{F_1}{5}$

Here, F_2 is the force exerted by the person on the crowbar to lift the force F_1, which is half the weight of the beam. If F_1 is 500 pounds, then the person using the crowbar exerts only 500 divided by 5 (100 pounds) of force to lift his end of the beam.

Suppose, then, that you move the fulcrum to the center of the crowbar. You will then need to exert the same force to raise the log as if you had no crowbar.

Now you know how to position your crowbar and fulcrum. The less distance between the fulcrum and the load-bearing end of the crowbar, the less force *you* will have to exert.

You can make use of this short course in mechanics in yet another way. Suppose you are building a fairly rough log shed of large, heavy beams, as we did last summer. (See "Equipment Shed") The wall of your building is by now five courses high. You have several more courses of logs to add, but they are too heavy for you to raise both ends simultaneously to the necessary height. You can manage with help to raise one end of the log, though. Fine. Once you've lifted one end of the log so that it rests on the top of the wall, you can then slowly slide it so that one-fourth of the log hangs over the wall. The wall now carries twice as much weight as a person on the lower end of the log would need to raise it. Or, to put it another way, the person must carry only one-third the total weight rather than one-half. If the log weighs 600

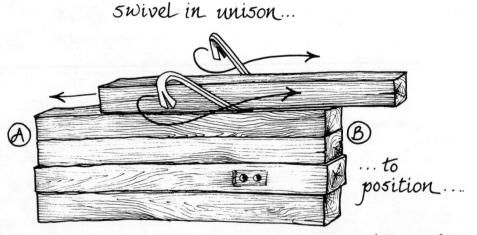

swivel in unison...

... to position ...

... moving points of crowbars toward Ⓐ and handles toward Ⓑ to move beam toward Ⓐ

pounds, the wall supports 400 pounds. Two people can easily heave up the remaining 200 pounds. Once the log rests on the wall, sliding it up is easy, and with several helpers, you can pivot it around in place.

If a beam is on the top course but hangs over at one end, have one person with a crowbar stand on each side of the wall. Insert the thin end of the crowbar between logs 4 and 5, with the crowbar pointing toward end B. Swing, or swivel together, raising beam 5 slightly and moving the crowbar point in the direction of end A. (Crowbar handle will then move toward B.) You can position your wood very exactly using this method.

A Word About Body Mechanics

To do a good job, safely:

1. It is important to use tools properly. It is even more important to use your body properly, especially in doing heavy work. A little applied

Trench - digging
from inside - out

knowledge of body mechanics can often make a hard job easier and save you unnecessary backache and muscle strain.

2. When digging a hole or trench, use a pickax to loosen the soil. Save your back by standing in the trench and tossing soil out with a shovel rather than leaning over the hole.

3. Whenever possible, let your legs bear the brunt of lifting, rather than your arms. To lift a heavy weight, flex your knees and lower your body's

bracing
to
Lift

center of gravity, instead of bending at the waist and lifting the whole weight with your shoulders and arms. Learn to brace your feet and let the transfer of your weight from one foot to another exert a force that would otherwise come, less effectively, from pulling with your arms. As much as you can, support a heavy load with your shoulders or your back rather than your arms.

4. If you are working as a team to pull, push and lift, agree on a starting signal so that you are all exerting maximum effort at the same time. Mike gives out a karate-like yell, *"Ho-Whup!"* which has the double effect of telling us when to push (pull, roll or lift) and also of instilling spirit in the group. When you've worked together for a while, that signal, when you hear it, means "give it all you've got." Jobs that would be impossible for two people are often easy for four, working together.

People look at our equipment shed, built of massive old beams, and shake their heads. They can't figure out how the four of us, physically fit but by no means unusually muscular or athletic, could have built it. How did we ever maneuver those beams into place? We did it by making use of these natural laws that govern the way things work. It took a lot of effort, but at no time was it really a strain. We did not hurt our backs or mash our toes. (But we drew more than one sigh of relief!)

Chapter Six

The Woodbutcher's Tools

Good tools are necessary for satisfying work with wood. This is one area where we do not skimp. The difference between a cheap screwdriver and a more expensive one that has a good bond between handle and metal is not always apparent on sight. But when the weakly attached handle breaks after a short period of use, or the pliers don't mesh well, the cheap tool is revealed as no bargain after all. If you still need some basic carpenter's tools, we'd recommend you buy the best you can afford. Use either new or secondhand wood, but first-rate tools. Those are our priorities, anyhow.

Once you have built up a collection of tools, store them safely—not in a jumble in a box, but securely mounted on a wall rack or arranged on a shelf so that cutting edges are protected. A thin board with holes of various sizes drilled through it, attached to your workshop wall, will hold a large collection of screwdrivers, punches and such. Hammers and axes may be hung on double nails on the wall. Have a place for each tool, if possible, and return it there after use. This isn't a fussy rule; it's a time and temper saver. You can waste an awful lot of energy and time trying to round up stray tools before you can begin on a job.

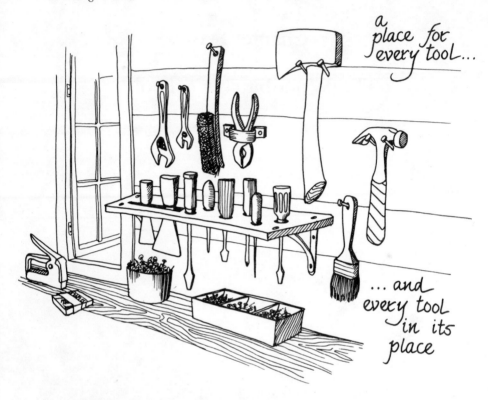

a place for every tool...

...and every tool in its place

If you keep your tools sharp, clean, well-oiled and free of rust, you will find that they are more of a pleasure to use. A cutting tool with a keen edge is safer to use than a dull one, since a person often tends to hack away in somewhat careless exasperation when a tool doesn't cut as it should. We consider a good bench grinder for sharpening tools an

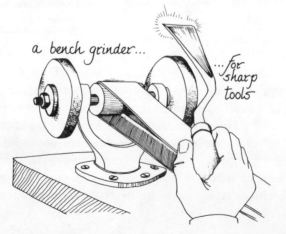

a bench grinder...

...for sharp tools

essential on our homestead. With the grinder, you need a dressing wheel to keep the grindstone in good shape. The wheel should be used solely to sharpen steel and hard iron—never lead, copper, aluminum or plastic, which will clog the stone with their fine dust.

Mostly, we avoid buying multi-purpose gadget tools, for we have found that they seldom do a truly good job of fulfilling all of their claimed functions.

The following list of basic tools includes nothing specialized or exotic. These were the implements we found necessary to build our barn, our most elaborate homestead building project:

- claw hammers
- 6-inch circular saw (portable)
- handsaws
  —carpenter's saws
  —bow saw
- rasp
- files
- screwdrivers
- crowbars—large and small
- pliers
- rubber mallet
- "Wunderbar"
- chisel
- carpenter's angle and T square
- adjustable wrench
- hacksaw
- 8-pound mallet
- cement trowel
- plumb line
- steel measuring tape
- folding measuring stick
- electric drill
- carpenter's pencil—or use nail for a scribe on rough lumber
- good level
- pickax

T. L. Gettings

Mike sharpening a hatchet in his workshop. This shows the fit of the salvaged window, which is hinged at the top. A hook prevents damage from the wind blowing the window.

ACCESSORIES

- stepladders
- 30-foot extension ladder
- carpenter's apron
- large-wheeled garden cart
- (rented cement mixer for barn foundation.)

Somes notes on individual tools:

CLAW HAMMERS are not all-purpose tools, although that is sometimes their fate. They should be used only for hitting nails and for removing them. Increase your leverage when removing nails by putting a small block of wood under the hammer head. If you have large spikes to be removed or boards to be pried apart, use a crowbar instead of a hammer. Heavy wrecking jobs can ruin a good hammer. Use as heavy a hammer as you can handle comfortably; it will strike the nail squarely and bounce around less than a lightweight hammer. Always look at the nail when hammering. Set the nail first with a few taps, then hit it hard with the hammer to drive it home.

CIRCULAR SAW—We found it worthwhile to use a carbide-tipped saw blade on our electric saw, especially with our used wood that sometimes contained unseen embedded nails. The carbide tip resists dulling if you accidentally buzz into a nail. If the carbide tip should break off, your local saw-sharpening expert may be able to replace it for you.

SAWS—A bow saw cuts more rapidly than a carpenter's saw, and in working with old lumber, which often frays easily, it is just as good. You will have to smooth the edges with a rasp in any case. In any cutting where accurate fit is important, bear in mind that (1) the saw removes a thin strip, wider than its blade, as it cuts the wood, and (2) the line that guides your cut should not waver at the edge of the board. It should be as straight as possible. A T square will help you here. A poorly directed beginning cut is next to impossible to correct as the saw bites deeper.

LEVEL—A poor level only lulls you into thinking that the boards are true; you find out differently later. When buying a level, check its accuracy by reading it right side up and then reversing it. The reading should be the same both ways. In using a level with old boards, watch out for surface irregularities on the wood that could throw you off. If possible, buy a short level for use in tight places and a 48-inch level for more accurate work on big jobs.

PLANES should always be stored resting on the side, never with the cutting edge down, or the blade will become chipped and dull.

DRILLS—We use an electric drill almost exclusively. A hand-held drill is more difficult to keep accurately on course.

FILES are for shaping metal. Filing, when done correctly, should leave a residue of thin, narrow shavings rather than metal dust. Soft metals

a tiny level

for tight spots

... and a bevel

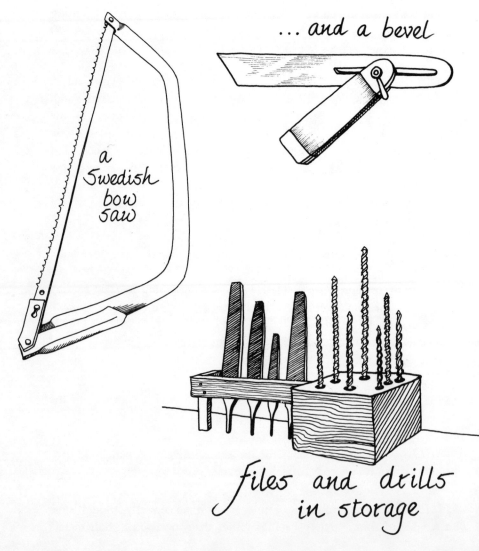

a
Swedish
bow
saw

files and drills
in storage

Rasps:

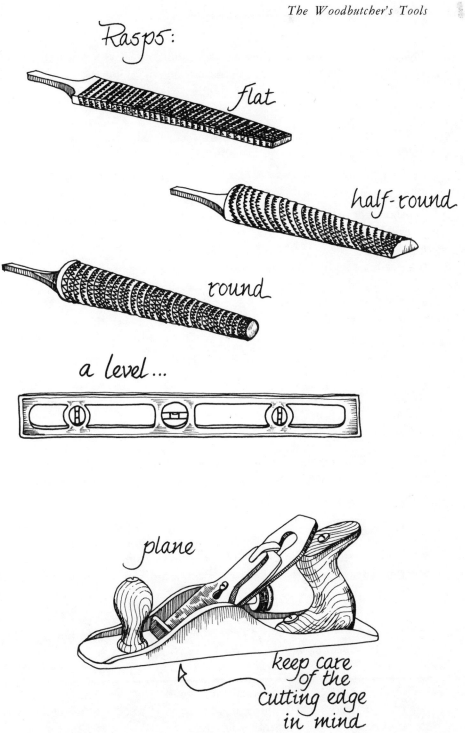

flat

half-round

round

a level...

plane

keep care
of the
cutting edge
in mind

like lead clog up files. We use a small paddle fitted with many short, stiff wires to clean our files. Never store files in a jumble. They are cutting instruments and will dull each other when rubbed together.

RASPS are good for shaping and smoothing wood. Keep a spare rasp blade handy and possibly a variety of shapes:

SCREWDRIVERS shouldn't be used to jimmy windows open, pry off paint-can lids or mark things. They should be used to drive screws. Buy yourself a variety of screwdrivers—always with thick, solid handles—so that you have the proper size for the screw you want to set: neither too big nor too small. Too wide a blade, used with a flathead screw, may mar the wood. Worse than too big is too small, for the edges of the screwdriver blade may wear off, and the tool may bend. A too-small screwdriver will also slip and wear out the edges of the groove in the screwhead, which will then make it difficult to get purchase on the screw even with an adequate-sized screwdriver.

RUBBER MALLET—Handy for "coaxing" jobs as well as for hitting wood that shouldn't be marred.

CHISEL—Like a plane, the chisel is a cutting tool that should be treated with respect, kept sharp and stored without knocking the blade on other surfaces.

"WUNDERBAR" is a tradename used for a 2-inch-wide, 12-inch-long, sharp-edged wrecking and prying bar. It is not as strong as a crowbar but the thin edge is very effective for prying boards apart or loosening banged-in nails.

MEASURING TAPES AND STICK—Just a hint: if you're buying a new one now, get one with metric markings.

CARPENTER'S PENCIL—Makes a good dark, thin, accurately placed line on your work. For rough-grained, darkened wood, we sometimes scribe a line with a nail for better visibility.

CARPENTER'S APRON—If you'll be doing a lot of nailing, this is a must. Ask for one when you buy hardware, cement or lumber. Many lumberyards and hardware stores give them free. Or make one out of old jeans, tarp or tent material.

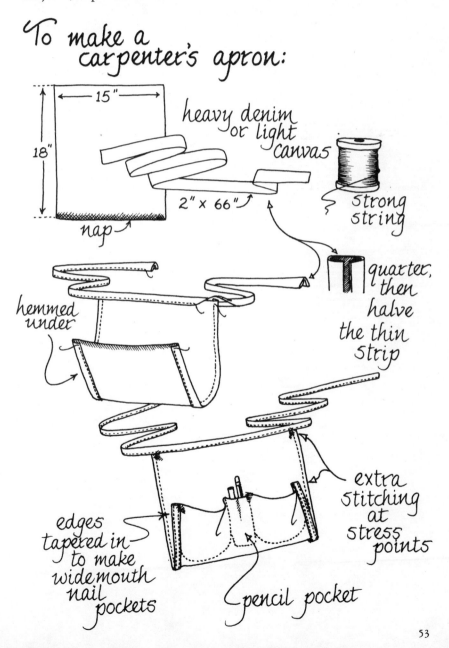

To make a carpenter's apron:

15"

18"

heavy denim or light canvas

2" x 66"

nap

Strong string

hemmed under

quarter, then halve the thin strip

edges tapered in to make widemouth nail pockets

extra stitching at stress points

pencil pocket

Chapter Seven

Construction

Some principles and some practical hints

As we see it, the important elements in building a satisfactory structure are these:

1. *A GOOD PLAN.* It's possible, we know, to knock together a doghouse or put up a freeform shelter without a formal plan, but we find that we get the best results when we sketch out, beforehand, the dimensions of the thing we intend to build. Doing this gives us a chance to plan the method of joining edges and to determine whether we do indeed have on hand lumber of the right size to complete the job. That's not to say that the plan doesn't change as we work on it, especially with big projects; it does, of course. But when we begin, we know where we are headed. It is sometimes worthwhile to make a scale model of a building you intend to construct, to give yourself a chance to see and solve structural problems in the three dimensions before you get to wrestling with heavy boards. Mike maps out our plans to scale on graph paper and usually runs through several versions before deciding on the one that seems right and final. The dimensions of the plan are often influenced by the sizes of wood that we have available. If you have many short pieces of lumber, for example, such as mill ends, you may want to make a many-sided building (polygon).

If you are planning to put up a building, you will also need to decide on a site. Consider convenience to the house, placement with reference to shade trees, suitability of location to the building's purpose, and probable appearance in relation to other structures in your home-stead compound. You don't want your new building to obstruct a pleasant view. Perhaps, on the other hand, it can serve as a windbreak or a background for espaliered fruit tree plantings. Most important of all, study the drainage situation around your proposed building. Picture what will happen in case of heavy snow or rain. Will the water run into the building's foundation, or will it drain off?

In setting the foundation of our barn into the side of a hill, we accepted a possible drainage problem, but forestalled trouble by em-bedding perforated plastic drainpipe in gravel around the edges of the foundation with another underground drain leading off from the end of the barn where soil level is lowest. Grading around a building can be a very effective method of controlling drainage. We once lived in an old house where heavy rain would sometimes leak into the basement. There was nothing wrong with the structure of the house, but the land immediately around the house sloped *toward* the foundation. Naturally,

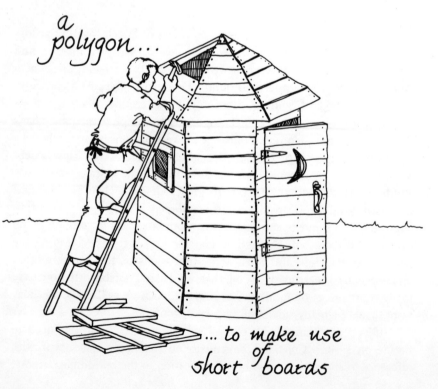

a polygon . . . . . . to make use of short boards

rainwater gravitated to the foundation and seeped through to the cellar. Grading (by hand with a shovel) so that land sloped away from the house, and digging a shallow trough to direct the rain, corrected the problem.

Building codes vary so widely, sometimes even within a single county, that it is impossible to give specific advice for complying with or circumventing these often reasonable, but also often unfairly restrictive, statutes. Our best advice to you is to find out about the building codes that apply in *your* community and to deal in a straightforward way with the people responsible for enforcing those codes. In many rural areas no permit is needed for putting up a building that is not a dwelling. If you run up against unreasonably narrow building codes, you might want to read *The Owner-Builder and the Code: Politics of Building Your Home* by Ken Kern, Ted Kogon and Rob Thallon.

2. *SOUND, APPROPRIATE MATERIALS.* Don't waste 2 by 6s in building a doghouse when one-inch tongue-and-groove siding would be adequate. Use nothing smaller than 2 by 4s for studs, and 2 by 6s for rafters in a conventionally framed building. Fir, pine and spruce make good rafters. There's nothing wrong with oak, but it's heavy to work with. You can make some substitutions, though. For example, when we were building our barn, we needed a strong beam to support a portion of the loft. Since we had not yet found our second source of used wood, the old barn that had to be taken down, we had no heavy beams. So we made a laminated beam by nailing two 2 by 10s together and then fastening a brace across them at intervals.

A material that is appropriate in a certain situation is not necessarily one that would be customary. We feel, for example, that our use of wood log rounds as building blocks to make our garage was an appropriate use for that material in our situation. We had the logs and needed a garage, so we used the logs in an unconventional but entirely satisfactory way.

One advantage of using recycled wood is that it is well seasoned. Most expert carpenters warn that building a permanent structure from green wood yields disappointing results. As the wood loses moisture, it will shrink and your well-levelled angles may shift. Nails driven into green lumber may loosen because the wood will shrink away from them. Lumber shrinks more in width than it does in length during the seasoning process because the cellulose fibers that, with lignin, make up the bulk of it, are arranged longitudinally. It is the moisture between these fibers that is lost when the wood is seasoned.

Sometimes it seems, though, that rules were meant to be broken, especially by us woodbutchers. As Larry Hackenburg relates in his book *The Green Wood House,* it *is* possible to build satisfactory, lasting structures of unseasoned wood, if you understand what's happening and work *with* the shrinkage. Board-and-batten siding, for example, with its built-in overlap, works very well with green wood. Hackenburg recommends using green oak, poplar, spruce, cypress or redwood.

We haven't built much with green wood ourselves, so we can't speak with any authority on this, but having read about Hackenburg's methods and results—four cabins and a house, at last report—we're certainly not about to say that it can't be done, and, apparently, done well.

If you are cutting lumber from your own trees, remember that boards cut from near the heartwood of the trees are more likely to warp as they season than those that are quarter-sawn from the outer wood.

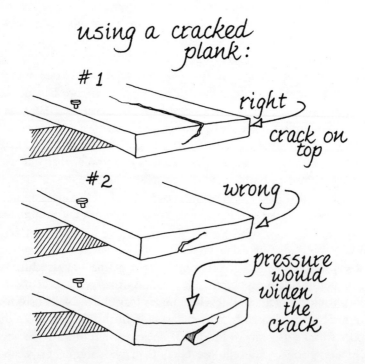

using a cracked plank:

#1

right

crack on top

#2

wrong

pressure would widen the crack

Packing crates and skids are often made of rough, green wood, which may warp and shrink after a season or two. They are perfectly good for many homestead construction projects, but should be used with full realization of their limitations.

Threaded and cement-coated nails hold better than plain ones and resist popping.

If you have some salvaged wood that has defects—knots, holes or splits—you can still use it if you will put it in a non-load-bearing part of your structure: an interior wall, hay manger or partition. All load-bearing wood should be sound, straight and well seasoned.

At this point, we should tell you what we do with a board that has a crack in it. There's no sense in pretending to each other that we'll never use imperfect wood. Most of us do, at one time or another. Why not, then, pay some attention to the best way to use it? Suppose you have a one-inch plank that has a crack in it, like this:

The plank is otherwise sound and too good to waste. You'd like to use it for flooring. How can you place the wood so as to minimize the weakening effect of the crack?

and using a cracked fence board:

this

not this

Keep the crack on top. Imagine a force pressing down on the crack in sketch #1. The force compresses the split wood, right? Now look at sketch #2. Force pressing on this plank would tend to widen the crack.

Now let's suppose that you have 1-by-8-inch plank that you want to use for board fencing. It has a crack on the edge. Keep in mind that a fence, especially a board fence, is likely to be subjected to some pressure from people climbing on it. You've no doubt already figured out the best placement for a cracked fence board for the reasons described above.

3. *CAREFUL CONSTRUCTION*. Since we build to please ourselves, you would find that one of our goat pen partitions is still embellished with a 1939 license plate that was nailed to the board in its previous existence as part of a big bank barn, or that the garage roof is low, or that part of the barn loft is left unplanked (purposely so, to allow for lumber storage).

We follow our own plans, but we try to do a sound job. That means a solid foundation, strict leveling, accurate squaring of corners and ample bracing. Whatever you build, take the time to do it right as you go along. If its falls apart in a year, repairs will likely be put off because, if your homestead is anything like ours, you'll be knee-deep in six more urgent homestead projects that you simply must complete between haying, canning and stacking the winter's wood. Whatever you're making, give it your full attention and your best workmanship. Trust your impulses—to use a piece of gnarled wood for a door handle, or old oak pegs as tool hangers—but attach them well and make your work solid.

We hope the following pointers will be of some help to you in putting up a sound building, from the ground up:

Foundation—A permanent, closed building like a barn or a house needs a firm foundation, dug deeply enough so that the footing on which the foundation rests, or the posts that support the frame, will be below frost level for your area. Footings are important. They bear the load of the building and transfer that weight to the soil below. Ideally, they should be made of poured concrete. For our barn we used rocks from the farm covered with a soupy concrete mixture poured into a form. The foundation, of concrete blocks, was squared by running strings between stakes set at each corner. Corners were laid down first. To check squaring of corners, measure the diagonal lines running from one corner to its opposite. If the corners are square, the lines will be the same length. To check an L-shaped building, divide it into component rectangles.

For a smaller, more open or dirt-floored building like a toolshed or three-sided equipment shed, you can get away with a less elaborate foundation if you are able to position your building in a spot where water will drain off in all directions. For example, our toolshed, situated on a barely perceptible crest that sheds rain on all sides, rests on concrete blocks set under each corner. There is no excavated foundation. The structure has stood in that place for about six years, and it shows no sign of settling yet. In a wet, poorly drained area, though, expansion of the greater amount of soil moisture could heave the ground and misalign the building.

Our equipment shed, a three-sided building constructed of heavy logs, sits on footings made of double concrete blocks, anchored with concrete set in excavations as deep as necessary to level the building, but not dug below the frost line. The building is more "loose jointed" than a conventional framed structure; a little shifting won't hurt it. We provided for good drainage by (1) running a gutter along the west (high) side under the roof with a downspout leading to the sloping drive, (2) digging a trench on the uphill side of the shed to direct water away from the building, and (3) grading and packing soil around the concrete piers so that water will drain off, not down around the concrete blocks.

Walls—In either log cabin-type or conventional stud framing, walls bear the weight of the roof. A pole building, with the framing poles sunk 4 to 6 feet in the earth, offers a versatile kind of construction in which the walls need not bear weight. The poles support both walls and roof. They are able to carry more weight than you might expect since they gain support for their load from the ground packed around them.

In erecting a studded wall of any kind, there will be stages in construction before the wall is tied in to other members, when it will be wobbly. Anchor the framing work by nailing a long piece of scrap wood as a brace between the free wall and a stable part of the building or beam on the ground. Level and square all corners before making the final attachment.

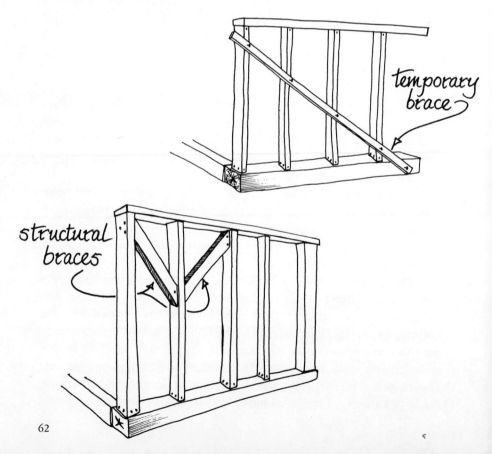

temporary brace

structural braces

Bracing of corners is important too, especially on the side of the structure that bears the brunt of the prevailing winds. Wind turbulence at corners (observe snow patterns) makes them vulnerable to shaking and consequent instability. Use only sound lumber for braces.

We used oak 2 by 6s to brace 4-by-4 corner posts in our barn.

To paint or not to paint? That's up to you. Unpainted wood will last better than a lifetime *if* there are no pockets of peeling paint or gouged out crevices where rainwater would stand and rot the wood. When wood can drain and dry freely, it is amazingly durable. Painting, once begun, must be continued. When you are combining random boards to make a structure, a coat of paint can unify the building and gloss over surface imperfections that might be distracting.

When using tongue-and-groove, try to place the grooved boards so that they will drain, rather than retain, rainwater.

Roof—In most cases, the roof will be the most expensive part of your building. Salvaged rafters aren't hard to find, but it's not often that you can obtain enough scrap roofing for a building of considerable size. If you are offered used slate for roofing, inspect it carefully. Charming as it is, old slate is often brittle and not worth your time and trouble.

Aluminum roofing has the advantages of lasting the life of the building, resisting fire and weighing much less than shingles, therefore being easier to handle. You may get some minor leakage around the nails caused by uneven expansion of the wood framing and metal roofing. For this reason, aluminum roofing is more suitable for your outbuildings than it is for your house.

Roll roofing is relatively inexpensive. For a low-pitched roof, from 1 to 3 inches rise per foot, you should overlap one-half the width of each layer with the next layer you put down. The result of this wide overlap is a double layer of roofing that is pretty leakproof. A single layer of roll roofing, with just a few inches of overlap, will protect a slightly steeper roof, with 4 inches or more rise to the foot (four pitch).

A steep roof is more expensive and more difficult to lay than one with a low pitch, because it uses more board framing and allows less convenient footing. It may be your choice, though, if your area is sub-ject to heavy winter snow. If you have extra heavy rafters—3 by 6 rather than 2 by 6—and space them no more than 24 inches apart, you will need less pitch. (The added width increases the strength of the board by squaring, not simple addition.) In a barn, especially one with

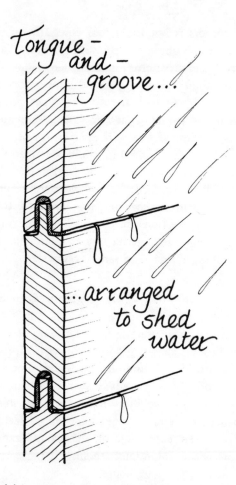

a metal roof, rising animal heat will loosen snow so that it seldom accumulates dangerously.

When using post and beam construction, you will most likely build your roof as soon as your posts are in the ground. When we built our barn, although it was of stud and beam construction, we finished the roof before putting the siding on, so that we could move the animals in and store hay in the loft. We were conscious, though, of the danger of wind turbulence in such a large roofed-over open area. You know what happens when you try to carry a 4-by-8 piece of plywood in a stiff breeze. Multiply that by our large roof surface and you will see that the wind could easily have picked up part of that roof and sent it sailing. So we hurried to complete the siding before doing any further interior finishing on the barn, and we'd advise you to do the same.

Chapter Eight

Butchery and Joinery

We hope that the following observations and reminders will save you some time and temper—possibly even materials—when cutting, nailing and screwing.

CUTTING

1. When making a deep cut with a saw, avoid exerting too much pressure on the saw or it may cut at an angle or go into one side of the wood, making a bulge.

2. To rip a long, thin board when doing rough work, try scoring the board at intervals up the width desired, and chop away the scored-off sections with an ax.

3. When cutting the end from a board, support the piece you're taking off, especially if it is heavy, so that it won't splinter the edge of your good board. Or have a helper do this.

NAILING

1. As you know, nails increase in diameter with the increasing numbers of their designation. Each gauge number is available in different kinds of nails: casing, box, common, finishing, cut, and so on.

score...

and chop away

Support from a friend...

...prevents splitting at end

T. L. Gettings

Mike scoring a board to even depth to prepare it for ripping by hand with a hatchet.

Greg Bubel

Mike and Nancy preparing a board.

2. Use thinner nails for hardwood than for softwood.

3. Galvanized, aluminum or copper nails resist weather.

4. Zinc- or cement-coated nails resist popping, but are difficult to withdraw.

5. If you suspect that the wood you're working with will split easily, try nailing some scrap wood of the same kind, the same distance from the edge as you intend to nail your work.

6. If wood splits when nailing, dull the nail point; if splitting continues, use a thinner nail. A dull nail makes a larger hole in the wood than a sharp one, though, and it may loosen more easily. This is another of those trade-offs. You dull the nail to solve one problem, but in so doing you may be creating another. You must weigh the different sides of the question. There's no one absolutely correct way to do the job. That's what woodbutchery is all about.

7. How many common nails are in a pound? Approximately the following:

2d nails...876
5d nails...271
7d nails...161
9d nails...96—on up to 60d spikes...11

nails angled

for a better hold

8. Get more nails than you think you'll need. We prefer to be slightly oversupplied than to find it necessary to run out to the hardware store in the middle of a job. This is all the more true if you're doing your woodbutchery on weekends, since most builders' supply stores seem to close at noon on Saturday.

9. Driving nails into wood at an angle makes a stronger tie than driving them perpendicularly. The two connected boards are less likely to pull apart. It is often easier, too, to drive a nail at an angle.

10. When nailing a board at two ends, drive the nails in different directions and they will hold better, especially if the object—like a sawhorse—will be pulled or picked up from the top.

11. If the wood you're working with has a coarse grain, like that of rapidly grown pine, drive the nail at an angle to the grain rather than with the grain or perpendicular to the grain, to avoid splitting.

SCREWING

1. Screws are sized by both shank diameter and length. Different lengths, ranging from ¼ inch to 5 inches, are available in each thick-

screw lengths:

not enough

at least ½ length

ness. (Not a full range, though; #2 screws come in ¼- and ½-inch lengths, and #7 in ½-to-1½-inch lengths, and #16 in 1¼-to-3-inch lengths, for example.

2. A screw should be long enough for at least one-half, and preferably two-thirds of its length to penetrate the base board into which it is driven.

3. Use finer threaded screws for hardwood than for softwood.

a
screw-starter

4. Start a hole for a screw to be driven into with a drill, a punch or a screw-starter (like a small corkscrew on a handle.)

5. Before inserting screws, rub the threaded tip in a bar of soap to make the screw drive more easily.

As the old carpenter told his helper,
Measure twice . . . . and you'll only have to saw once!

PART II

One Way to Make a Garage

The nice thing about using what's available to make what you need is that you end up with a product unlike any other. Often it has a vitality of its own, a rightness for your place, that could never have come off an assembly line.

Take our garage, for example. Our 91-acre farm had only a house and small shed when we bought it. We needed a shelter of some sort to try to extend the life of our car for a few more years. Yet we didn't want to go to the expense of putting up a conventional garage; we preferred to invest in planting fruit trees and improving the fields. We were not really sure, either, about the choice of a permanent location for such a building, since we were still feeling our way into the farm, trying to fit each new project in harmoniously with the whole, and reluctant to put up some glaring new eyesore we'd regret later.

It was well into the fall, and we knew we'd be needing winter shelter for our car, but we were too busy to give the matter much conscious thought. We were intent on preparing to build a pond in our lower field, clearing an acre of thick brush and trees so that the pond dimensions could be accurately laid out. The last tree to go, at the edge of this field, was a giant willow with three massive trunks leaning over what would someday be the pond. (And now is.) Each trunk of the tree was 20 to 24 inches in diameter. Mike and our friend Charlie cut the trunks from the base, using chain saw and wedges. The three thuds reverberated clear up to the house, two fields away. The next step

Mike Bubel

As you can see, the garage is really a large, well-stacked and stabilized woodpile, roofed over, with firewood stacked beside it and bean poles leaning against the far end. The slope of the garage roof drains off rain and the overhang on the right helps to keep an extra stack of wood dry.

Large wood rounds, mixed with those of smaller diameter, form a tight, stable wall for the garage, seen here from the east (highest) side.

Mike Bubel

was to slice the logs into 15-to-24-inch hunks that could at least be rolled, if not lifted, to remove them from the site.

We rolled the hefty chunks of willow over to the waiting tractor and wagon, then up a log-supported scrap-wood ramp onto the wagon. Their destination was the woodpile near the house, where they would be split for firewood. (Willow isn't one of your great heating woods, far from it, but it does season quickly and provides a cheerful fire during the cool days of fall and spring when you want the atmosphere but not the heat.)

As it turned out, though, we didn't burn those big willow rounds. We built our garage of them. It took many trips to bring all of the pieces of tree up from the pond site. Somewhere along the way, we began to think of our big woody chunks as building blocks. No longer an obstacle to the building of the pond, they became a valued resource.

77

Build a garage out of willow chunks? We played around with the idea for awhile, until finally Mike said, "We can do it!" And we did. We stacked up the big willow rounds, cut side out, just like a large woodpile, and made ourselves a garage. Here's how we did it:

After much debate about the site, we chose to tuck the garage behind the woodpile wall that stretched between the old stone outdoor fireplace (part of a long-gone summer kitchen) and a tree. The structure has three sides and a roof, with the fourth, open side facing away from the west wind that prevails here.

First we laid down a track of long-lasting locust and cedar scrap wood where the walls would be, to protect the first course of logs from ground moisture. Then we piled the wood rounds on this base to form three walls. The base of the walls is composed of half-rounds of the willow (pieces so big they had to be split for ease of handling).

After the first course of wood half-rounds was positioned, we built up the walls chunk by chunk, using the wood pieces as though they were building blocks. We set the largest pieces first, on the lower part of the walls. We had plenty of wood to choose from, so we were usually able to select just the right round for a particular gap.

And how did we maneuver those outlandishly big logs into place without wrecking our backs? Well, for one thing, willow is a very lightweight wood. Oak, locust or hickory logs of that size would have been difficult, if not impossible, for us to handle. And secondly, we did very little lifting. We rolled the logs. We rolled the big base halves, end over end, and levered them into place using a crowbar or a piece of

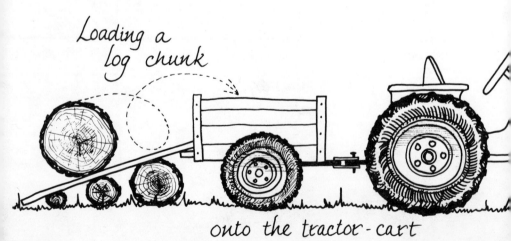

Loading a log chunk

onto the tractor-cart

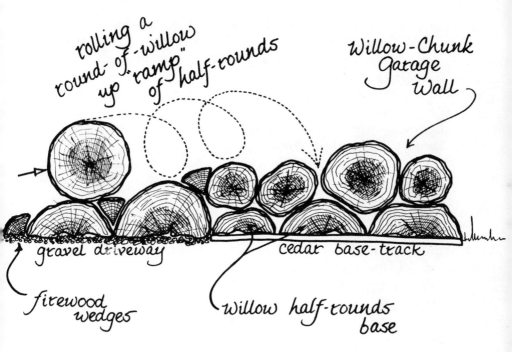

rolling a round-of-willow up "ramp" of half-rounds

Willow-Chunk Garage Wall

gravel driveway

cedar base-track

firewood wedges

willow half-rounds base

lumber. The next course was easy, for the halved log made a natural ramp. We selected the log to be put in the farthest corner and, rather than lift it into place, we rolled it up and over the first course of logs. Sturdy work gloves help here, as does a sense of timing—one, two, three, roll! And the log obeys. Almost too easy. Well, not really. Sometimes we'd get stuck. Logs wouldn't always end up neatly poised between the two rounds of the previous row and we'd have to jimmy them over. Or a log would have an awkward bump that made it hard to place. Mostly, though, it was a very satisfying job.

For succeeding courses of the garage walls, we set progressively smaller logs. Still, there were many wood rounds on the third and fourth courses that were too heavy or awkward to lift but just right for rolling. To get these big pieces up to the level where we wanted them, we simply placed several rounds and half-rounds of the willow, graduated in size, at the end of the garage wall to form a rather bumpy "ramp." We rolled the logs up this incline and then across the top row of set-in-place logs to their appointed places.

No mortar was used. The wooden cylinder blocks are 18 to 24 inches thick (cut edge to cut edge) and fit together firmly. After all the big pieces were in place, we went around chinking gaps with sticks and small logs to form a kind of wood mosaic effect. On the last course of logs we used a variety of smaller 2-to-8-inch diameter pieces that fit together closely.

To pitch the roof enough to allow for good drainage, we made the wall by the woodpile 6 feet 8 inches high, sloping to the outer long wall which is 9 inches lower. The open space enclosed by the walls is 8 feet wide by 15 feet long.

We set the eleven rafters in position, placing them directly on the garage walls. The rafters used were 2 by 6s from the brooder house we'd had wrecked for us, left from the pile of recycled wood we had used to build our barn. In order to stabilize the rafters, Mike took 2-to-3-foot lengths of oak furring strips, also left from the barn project, and nailed them vertically to both the rafters and the cut faces of several logs. On top of the rafters Mike nailed sheets of used exterior grade half-inch plywood left from the brooder house and, on top of the plywood, asphalt roofing strips purchased by the roll for $25.00—our only expense, other than nails, in building the garage.

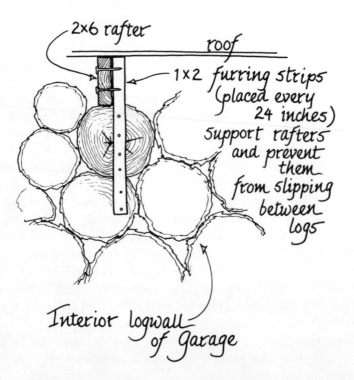

2×6 rafter

roof

1×2 furring strips (placed every 24 inches) support rafters and prevent them from slipping between logs

Interior logwall of garage

Anyone who needs a sheep hut, range shelter, woodshed, tractor shed or even outhouse, and has plenty of large logs but no sawmill, could follow this same method to build the structure right out on the field, entirely by hand labor except for the hauling of the logs. For extra snugness, the spaces between the logs could be chinked with moss.

The large size of the logs gives the structure stability. Thinner, fireplace-size logs would need more fastening and support to keep them standing securely.

We don't expect the garage to last forever. Frankly, we don't know what its useful life span will be. Fifteen years or so seems a reasonable expectation. It may last much longer than that. The whole idea of the structure, though, was to use what we had to meet an immediate need, to have fun doing it, and not to worry too much about things. The garage has so far weathered three winters and looks quite permanent. We've stacked fireplace wood along its three walls, making it snugger than ever. It looks, in fact, like a structure from Middle Earth— hunched, chunky, woody, slightly lopsided, with room for huddling Hobbits and Trolls left under the overhanging eaves.

Willow - Chunk Garage

asphalt roofing over half-inch plywood over 2×6 rafters

30" overhang

6½'   9½'   5½'

stacked firewood

81

Tractor Cart

Sometimes a simple device, well built, can serve many different purposes on a small farm. Our tractor cart, for example, is one of our most useful pieces of heavy farm equipment, second only to the tractor. We use the cart for everything from hauling manure, to loading hay, to collecting firewood, to delivering log sections to our nearby sawmill. Its usefulness is far out of proportion to its cost, its size, or its elegance of design, but the very simplicity of it accounts for much of its versatility. The cart is simply the entire rear wheel assembly of an old car or truck, complete with the drive shaft, topped by an eight-foot wooden box body. The body is a three-sided box, with grooves in the sides at each end to hold two removable end panels. Two upright iron straps welded to the axle provide a base for bolting the cart body onto the wheel assembly. A double iron tongue, with a $\frac{3}{4}$-inch eye at one end, welded to the drive shaft, makes it possible to attach the cart to the tractor's drawbar. By inserting a hitch pin through the double eye and a drawbar hole, we can link the cart to the tractor hitch.

Countrymen have been making carts like these for years, with many local variations depending on what they had available. This cart is not of our design. It was put together by Henry Newland, who owned and loved this farm for many years, and who was kind enough to tell us how he made his cart.

The tractor cart in use for hauling firewood.

Mike Bubel

MATERIALS:
Rear car or truck wheel assembly with tires and drive shaft.
Angle irons and steel plates.
Bolts.
Wood—tongue-and-groove preferred, two 4 by 4s 8 feet long, eight 2 by 4s 3 feet 9 inches long.
Sixteen 3-inch-by-6-inch angle irons.

METHOD:
Take the wheel assembly to a welder and ask him to weld two L irons (approximately 3 inches by 6 inches) to the axle, one on each side, to support the wagon bed. Have him, also, attach two 1-inch steel pipes to both the axle and the drive shaft, as shown in the diagram. He should then weld a double steel plate, pierced by a ¾-inch hole, to the end of the drive shaft, so that the wagon can be attached to the tractor's drawbar.

The rest of the wagon construction is up to you. Bolt an 8-foot 4 by 4 to each large angle iron that is welded to the axle. Next bolt

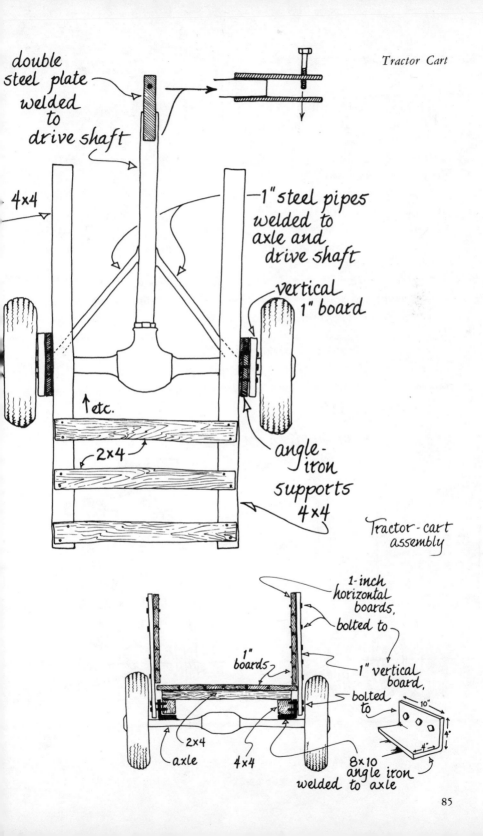

double
steel plate
welded
to
drive shaft

4x4

1" steel pipes
welded to
axle and
drive shaft

vertical
1" board

↑etc.

2x4

angle-
iron
supports
4x4

Tractor-cart
assembly

1-inch
horizontal
boards,
bolted to

1" boards

1" vertical
board,
bolted
to

2x4

axle

4x4

10"

4"

4"

8x10
angle iron
welded to axle

eight 2 by 4s at 14-inch intervals (O.C.) to the 4 by 4s. Support each 2 by 4 with an angle iron bolted to both the 2 by 4 and the 4 by 4.

Now the final step in making the wagon bed: nail tight-fitting boards (tongue-and-groove preferred) to the 2-by-4 supports to form the floor of the wagon bed.

To attach sides to the cart, bolt a 1-by-10 board (or a steel plate) to the large angle iron that is welded to the axle. Cut one-inch lumber to fit the length of the wagon and bolt it to the upright one-inch board or steel plate, whichever you choose to use. Tongue-and-groove lumber is a good choice for the sides.

Attach two 1-inch cleats, leaving a one-inch groove between them, at both front and rear ends of each side of the cart, to secure the front and back removable ends, which are made by bolting 1 by 4s to two 1 by 2s.

Keep the wagon bed swept clear of hay, chaff, manure and any other such material that might prevent prompt draining and drying of rainwater, and it should last for years, even if kept outside.

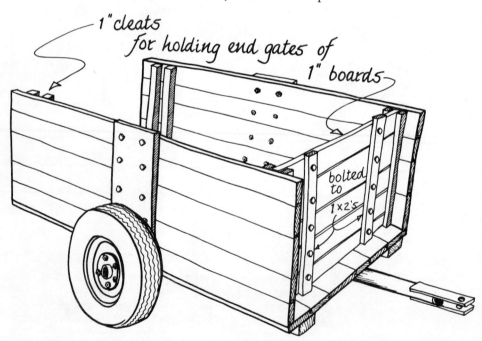

1" cleats
for holding end gates of
1" boards

bolted to 1 x 2's

Sawhorse

A sturdy, portable work surface is a real help in carrying out many large and small homestead projects. This wide-saddled sawhorse that Mike made serves many purposes. One of its best features is that it can support a small board on its wide top, making a hand sawing job easier and safer than it would be with the use of conventional sawhorses. (It makes a good perch for barn visitors who come at milking time, too!)

To make Mike's wide-saddled sawhorse, you'll need a 2 by 8 about 28 inches long, four 2 by 4s 30 inches long, two pieces of 1/2-inch plywood about 15 by 10 inches, and two 1/2-inch-by-2-inch braces.

In the sawhorse that Mike made for himself, both the 2 by 8 top surface and the 2 by 4s that fit into its four corners are bevelled for an interlocking fit. That's not absolutely necessary, though; Mike just likes to make intricate cuts and see them fit together. If you want to make a simpler version of our wide sawhorse, but one that will be sturdy enough for plenty of heavy use, nail the 2 by 4s to the narrow edges of the 2 by 8 as shown in the diagram, rather than bevelling and joining the edges of these pieces as Mike did. For best stability, the angle where the sawhorse legs join the top should be no less than 15 degrees.

Mike's Sawhorse

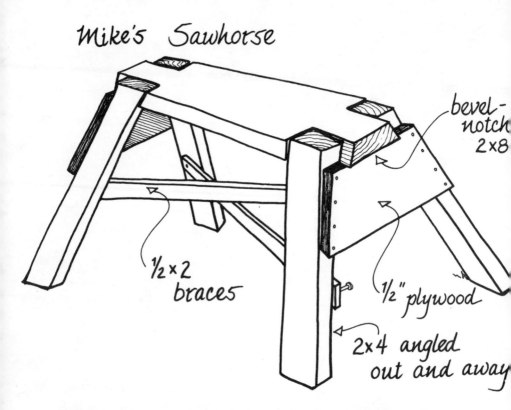

bevel-notch 2×8

½ × 2 braces

½" plywood

2×4 angled out and away

Sawhorses: conventional type on the left, Mike's workbench/sawhorse on the right.

T. L. Gettings

T. L. Gettings

Mike sawing a board on his wide-topped sawhorse.

stabilized
by
crossbraces
and end
boards

Simpler-to-make
Sawhorse

Sawbuck

A sawbuck is a sawhorse with extended arms. The arms hold wood in place for ease in sawing logs. If you cut fireplace logs or stove wood, a sawbuck will make the job faster and easier. Simply position the log in the V of the upward-extending arms and saw away!

The sawbuck is especially useful for cutting sapling wood with a bow saw. We never return from the woods empty-handed. If we've found nothing else to bring, we usually trudge back dragging a well-seasoned dead cedar or other small tree for firewood. These 1-to-3-inch diameter sticks are piled near the sawbuck and when Mike has a few minutes before the dinner bell rings, he'll saw off a few for the next morning's fire.

Our sawbuck, in true woodbutcher tradition, is made of what we had—3-inch cedar poles for arms, braced with 1-by-3 boards from snowmobile crates.

You can make a sawbuck in a morning, and have time left over before lunch to do some sawing. First, cut your braces and end pieces the length you want them to be. Our sawbuck is 42 inches long. (Too short a sawbuck will be wobbly; too long a one, and the braces won't be rigid enough. But there's a good bit of room for variation between these extremes.)

Next, smooth the logs flat at the point where they will cross. Mike chipped them with an ax and then smoothed the surface with a rasp. If you use 2 by 4s, of course, you can omit this step.

Nancy Bubel
Mike cutting a log to fireplace length on the sawbuck.

Sawbuck

3-inch
cedar poles

13"

34"

2x3's

1x3's

42"

Nail the end pieces together in a big X, a top-heavy X with the longer arms extending upward rather than downward. Nail a short 1-by-3 brace between the lower ends of each X. Then nail upper and lower braces between the two crossed end pieces, finishing with a cross brace extending from lower left to upper right on each side of the sawbuck.

You may want to cut the feet of the sawbuck at an angle so that the device stands flat, especially if you intend to use it on a flat surface. On normally uneven ground, this step would not be necessary.

Then set up the sawbuck and use it. Save the sawdust for mulching your raspberries!

Hay Rake

Like many homesteaders, we make hay on our place largely by hand. We sometimes have a field of hay cut and baled by a neighbor, too, but there are always patches of special clover, odd-shaped small fields, or spots too wet to work with heavy equipment, where we like to do a "custom job." Until last year, we'd always used a hay fork and bamboo rake to gather the dried grass into windrows and then into piles. No more, though. Mike spent several rainy afternoons in his barn workshop making four hayrakes for us. What a difference! These wooden hay rakes, similar to those Mike used as a boy, are just the right tools for the job. They are light in weight, they rake a wide area, they catch even the small blades of grass and nutritious leaves, and they glide easily over the ground. The rakes are a pleasure to use. Each of our rakes is a different size. The 28-inch one is probably the most generally useful. Smaller sizes are good for children to use.

Mike used the following materials for each rake:

4 to 6 foot long, one-inch diameter rake handle, available at hardware stores.

One piece of 1-by-2-inch lumber, 20, 24, or 30 inches long.

Wood glue.   ⅜-inch doweling.   Two small nails.

Greg Bubel

Mike raking hay with wooden rake he made.

Mike Bubel

(Yes, we bought the rake handle new: imagine that!) If you have a nice straight, smooth pole in your woods, you could use that. Mike says that in Poland, people would usually use a good strong, one-inch shoot from the shrubby hazelnut tree for their handles. The hazelnut (or the domesticated filbert) produces many strong, slender limbs that do not taper but remain the same diameter throughout their length— good qualities for a rake handle.

To make the rake, cut ⅜-inch dowel into ten, twelve, or sixteen (for small, medium, or large rakes) 3½-, 4-, or 4½-inch lengths. These will be the rake teeth. Cut a 20-, 24-, or 28-inch long piece of 1-by-2-inch scrap wood, sand it smooth and drill ten, twelve or fourteen ⅜-inch holes in its wide surface. Drill a one-inch hole in the narrow surface of the rake head to accept the handle. Mike made pointed teeth for the rake by chipping one end of the dowels with a chisel. Glue a dowel into each hole in the rake head, using wood glue. Glue the handle into the hole on the rake head. Allow to dry before handling.

Drill two ⅜-inch holes at a 45-degree angle on the rake head, each 3½, 5½ and 7½ inches (O.C.) from the handle. Measure a 6½-, 7½-, or 13½-inch piece of ⅜-inch diameter dowel and cut one end of the dowel at an angle so that it will butt the rake handle. Chip away the rounded surface of the handle at the point where the dowel-brace will rest.

Then glue the dowel brace into the hole and to the flat spot on the rake handle. Finish by driving a small nail through the dowel brace into the handle.

RAKE DIMENSIONS:	Small Rake	Medium Rake	Large Rake
Number of Teeth	10	12	14
Length of Dowel Support	6½″	7½″	13½″
Length of Rake Teeth	3½″	4″	4½″
Rake Head Length	20″	24″	28″
Handle Length	±4 ft.	±5 ft.	±6 ft.

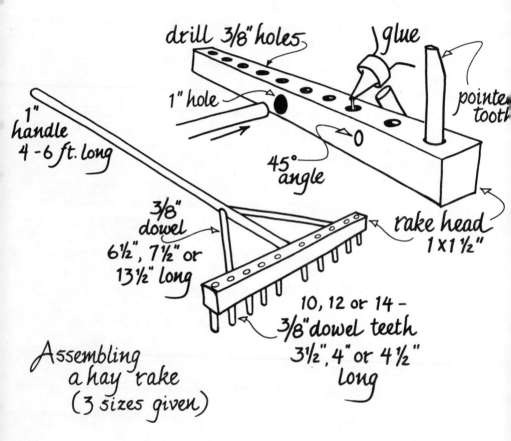

drill 3/8" holes

glue

1" hole

pointe
tooth

1"
handle
4 - 6 ft. long

45°
angle

O

3/8"
dowel
6½", 7½" or
13½" long

rake head
1 × 1½"

10, 12 or 14 –
3/8" dowel teeth
3½", 4" or 4½"
long

Assembling
a hay rake
(3 sizes given)

Sifting Screen

An assortment of lap-sized sifting screens will have many uses on the homestead, from sizing sunflower seeds to winowing chaff from grain to sifting compost. You may want to make one with fine wire screening and several more with different grades of coarse hardware cloth.

Either make a four-sided bottomless box, or knock the slats or corrugated cardboard base out of the bottom of a cantalope crate, as we did. Cut your screening two inches wider than the width of the open side of the bottomless box. Stretch the screening taut across the bottom

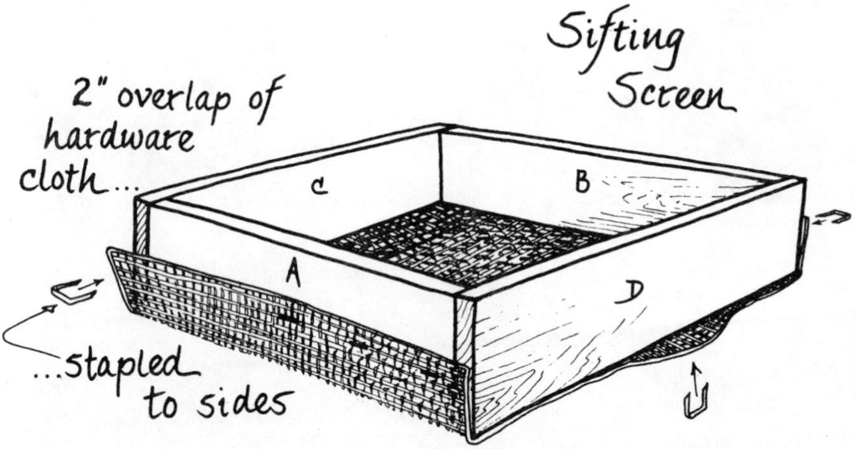

2" overlap of hardware cloth...

Sifting Screen

...stapled to sides

T. L. Gettings

Mike sifting seeds through a homemade winnowing screen. Chaff remains on top of hardware cloth.

of the box and staple it to the side of panels A and B and to the bottom edge of the side panels C and D.

You know what? This is the easiest project in this book. Make it the day after you build the barn.

Small Animal Creep

A creep is a special, limited-access shelter for baby animals, usually with a low entrance to keep out older stock. The creep may be a structure or simply a fenced-off area, as long as it serves its purpose of allowing young animals to rest and feed, undisturbed by their rowdier elders.

There is much to be said for making a little box shelter creep, which is what we've done. The arrangement is then portable and the box is low enough to serve as an exercise platform for young goats, who need muscular activity for proper development. The baby goats consider this little box creep to be their home, and it is a comical sight to see several of them peering from the doorway with a proprietary air. They jump on top of the box, frolic on it, and leap from it with those sideways twists that only carefree goats seem able to execute. We use the box as a warming shelter for very young kids while they are still in their own pen, and then move it to the goat loafing area when the babies are big enough to share quarters with the older goats.

The box is a simple and traditional design. The important things about it are that:

1. All wood edges should be smoothly sanded to eliminate splinters, and nails should be removed from used wood.

2. The structure should be sound enough to support even an adult goat.

T. L. Gettings

Kids play on and in their creep. Slats to the left form one wall of the hen pen.

3. The doorway should be restricted—we use a board across both the top and the bottom—to keep out nosy older goats (or sheep), leaving an entrance that only a kid or lamb will fit through.

4. The roof should be broad and smooth, because it will be used as a lounging platform.

5. The roof of the box should be as low as possible to conserve the kids' or lambs' body heat in cold weather. (Warm air rises.)

Mike used 1-inch tongue-and-groove and short pieces of 2 by 2 and 1-inch board to make the kid creep. It has four sides, no floor, and an entrance restricted by horizontally nailed boards.

To make the creep, first assemble the two sides by nailing 1-inch tongue-and-groove horizontally to two 2-by-2 corner posts. Nail a 1-by-3-inch brace in the center of each side panel.

Then nail boards across the back, joining the two sides.

Next nail the top and bottom boards across the front entrance.

Now nail the roof boards to a 1-by-4 center brace and then to the sides.

Finally, smooth all sharp edges with rasp or coarse sandpaper.

Creep for Young animals

Goat Exercise Platform

Goats are active, playful and intelligent animals. They appreciate having a little furniture around to make life interesting. This climbing platform hideout that Mike devised serves many purposes in the loafing pen. It is almost constantly in use.

• Jumping on and off the platform gives the goats necessary exercise, especially important when they are confined to their pen in severe weather.

• Playing King of the Mountain on their sturdy perch is part of a social process that helps them to establish their own order within the herd.

• The view is better from the top of the platform. Goats are full of curiosity and consider it their duty to keep tabs on what the neighboring hens and sheep are up to, as well as who enters the barn, and why.

• Shy or weak goats often hide out in the cozy space enclosed by the platform.

While the platform may not have any direct effect on milk production, the goats enjoy it tremendously. What's a homestead for if you can't do a few things just for fun?

T. L. Gettings

Goat climbing/lounging platform. Note rounded edges and end braces.

The wide base of the platform gives it stability. If often holds three adult goats. The brace on each open end helps to prevent the boards from wobbling and shifting, as do the boards nailed vertically across the top and bottom of the open ends.

We used 1-inch tongue-and-groove and scrap boards and 1 by 6s, 1 by 4s and 1 by 3s to make the climber/hideout. Here again, it was important to have all wood surfaces smooth and free of nails, splinters or any other sharp projecting parts that might injure the goats.

Mike made the two sides and the top of the climber as individual units, nailing random-width boards of tongue-and-groove to 1 by 4s for the top, 1 by 6s and 1 by 3s for the sides, and then rasping the corners and edges. After assembling the sides and top, he nailed the diagonal brace across each end of the structure to keep the sides in the proper position, allowing for correct width at the top to accept the roof. Then he attached the bottom board across each open end. Finally, he nailed 1-inch tongue-and-groove boards to two parallel 1 by 4s to form the top.

Note that the boards that form the floor/roof of the climbing platform run the short way, rather than the long way, across the span. The shorter boards are more rigid and stand up better to the almost constant clatter of hooves than a longer board would.

Mike then completed the climbing platform by nailing the roof to the already assembled sides.

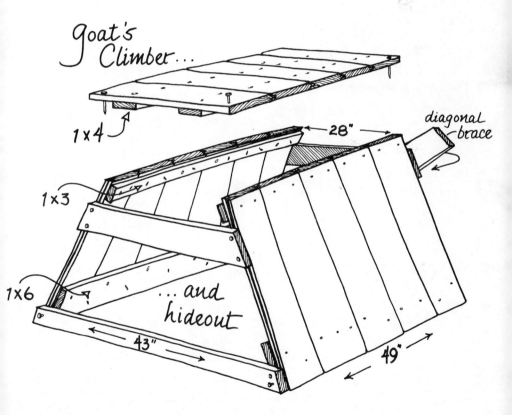

Goat's Climber...

1 x 4

1 x 3

1 x 6

... and hideout

28"

diagonal brace

43"

49"

Sheep Shelter

Sheep give so much and ask so little. They are ideal homestead animal partners. A well-fleeced sheep will have wool thick enough to plunge your fist into. Thus well insulated, she can stand a lot of cold if she has the basics of clean water, shelter at night and grain in winter.

The sheep shelter we are about to describe is useful year-round: as a sun shade and rain refuge in summer, night and day shelter in moderate cool weather, and daytime hideout in winter. During the winter we keep our flock in the barn at night and on very cold or stormy days, but when we do turn them out during the day, we are confident that they have a secure place to huddle should a sharp wind blow up.

Sheep often try to enter a narrow doorway two at a time. They like to have a place where they can take refuge and keep warm together. But at the same time, they like to enter and leave easily, often as a group. Therefore we made their shelter wide and tall at the opening, tapering to a lower-roofed, narrower closed wall opposite the opening. This trapezoidal shape gives the sheep both security and easy access. Chances of a lamb being trampled in the doorway are minimal. And, not so incidentally, the plan makes good use of the relatively short but sturdy pieces of 1-inch tongue-and-groove siding that we had on hand.

The structure sits well into the wind, with its tapered lower end. Because of its design, it is self-bracing. The shelter is more stable—less likely to wobble—than a rectangular structure would be, although it has slightly less usable floor space because of the angle of the side walls.

Sheep resting in sheep shelter.   *T. L. Gettı*

And it is readily transported, by pulling with a tractor or two strong people, to a different spot in the pasture. That is another reason for using the self-bracing design. Hauling an open shed around often loosens its joints and makes it unstable.

MATERIALS USED:

- Tongue-and-groove siding, recycled
- Nails
- 2 by 3s and 2 by 4s for base and framing

Another consideration in this and in any other buildings that will remain outside in the weather is that when tongue-and-groove lumber is used, it should always be placed in a vertical position so that water drains down the grooves and off the wood. Horizontally nailed tongue-and-groove is fine for structures that will be kept under cover, but you can readily see that water would tend to remain in those grooves rather than run off. In using secondhand tongue-and-groove in which there may be extra gouges, pieces of missing tongue or incomplete groove, the danger of wood rot from water standing in horizontal grooves would be even greater.

Here are directions for building the sheep shelter:

1. To make the sides, nail vertical tongue-and-groove (or other) siding to 2-by-4 (bottom) and 1-by-6 (top) crosspieces. (All 2 by 4 would be fine. Make use of what you have.)

2. Position sides at correct angle and nail on front and back bottom boards to stabilize the structure. Sometimes Mike nails a temporary brace between the two sides of a structure like this to hold the sides in the right position while he attaches the top and bottom crosspieces that will firm everything up. To check whether the sides are both set at the same angle, measure diagonally from B to D and C to A. If all is well, both measurements should be the same.

3. Continue to nail horizontal boards up the back of the shelter, letting the ends of the boards extend beyond the shelter sides and cutting them all off at once with a handsaw when the back is completely boarded up.

Sheep leaving shelter—as a group, as always!

T. L. Gettings

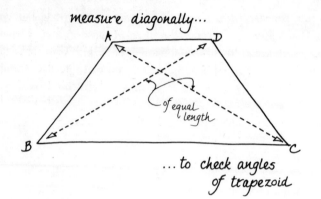

measure diagonally...

A   D

of equal
length

B   C

...to check angles
of trapezoid

Sheep Shelter
front view

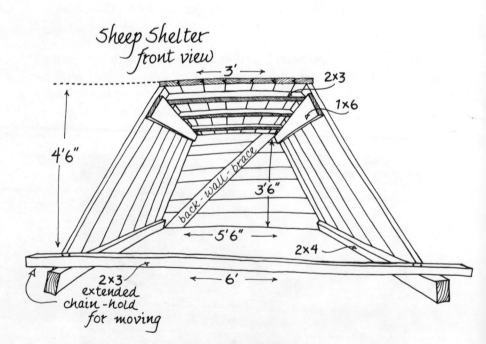

3'

2x3

1x6

4'6"

back-wall-brace

3'6"

5'6"

2x4

2x3
extended
chain-hold
for moving

6'

Side view...

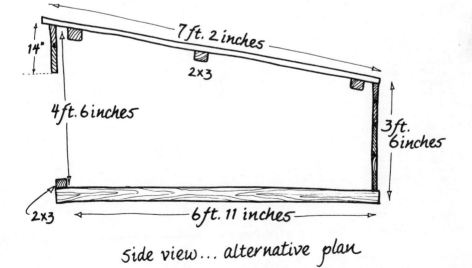

7 ft. 2 inches

14"

4 ft. 6 inches

2x3's

opening
faces
← south in winter;
← north in summer

3 ft.
6 inches

2x3

2 x 4

6 ft. 11 inches

... the way
we did it

7 ft. 2 inches

14"

2x3

4 ft. 6 inches

3 ft.
6 inches

2x3

6 ft. 11 inches

Side view... alternative plan

This makes it easier to get each board end cut at the right angle, so that the back is flush with the sides.

4. Allow the bottom board in front to extend a few inches beyond the sides of the shelter to provide a chain-hold when moving the shelter.

5. Nail on diagonal braces front and back.

6. Nail random width one-inch tongue-and-groove boards to three 2 by 3s to form the roof.

7. Fit the roof on top of the shelter and nail it in place.

Hay Mangers

A good manger should make hay easily available to the animals, while at the same time protecting it from contamination and waste. Goats are particular about their hay. They will turn up their noses at any that has been stepped on, touched by droppings, or even nosed over for too long. They also tend to waste a lot of hay if they can pull it out easily.

Keyhole or slatted mangers help to prevent wasted hay since, in order to reach the hay, the goat must feed with her head in the narrow space, making it difficult for her to suddenly withdraw a mouthful of your best alfalfa and drop it on the bedding. Such mangers also protect the hay from climbing kids and random droppings. They are less suitable for sheep, who have short, thick necks, and unnecessary for cows, who are less fastidious about their food.

There is an even easier way to build mangers, though, that has worked well for us. Our goat mangers are long box-like troughs made of scrap 1-inch tongue-and-groove siding. They are nailed to the framing posts of the pens, so that they extend into the aisle rather than into the animals' living area. The solid floor of the manger retains the nutritious leaves that shatter from the hay. The side of the manger near the aisle is 20 inches high, to accommodate the armloads of brush and coarse weeds that we sometimes feed the goats in summer. The side of the manger facing on the goat pen is slatted horizontally, so that the animals must reach their heads into the opening to get a good mouthful

T. L. Gettings

Mike in barn near goat pen—showing framing. Note slot at near end of manger for brushing out stale feed; brush hangs above the manger.

T. L. Gettings

Outdoor hay manger for the buck pen—supported by four cedar corner posts and protected by a sloping roof. Old tongue-and-groove boards form the deep manger bed—useful for piling brush and coarse weeds.

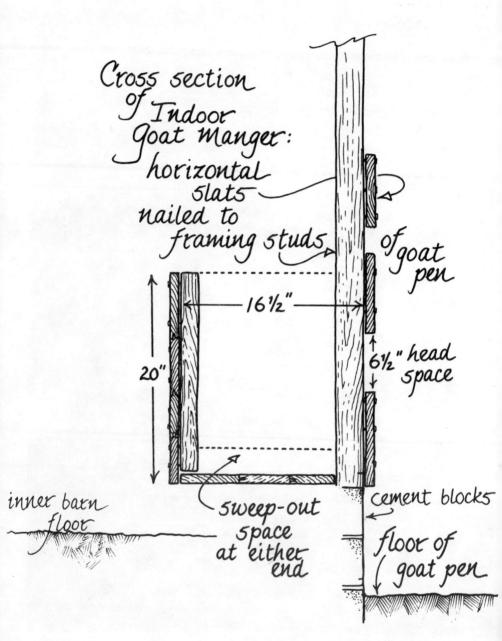

Cross section of Indoor Goat Manger: horizontal slats nailed to framing studs

of goat pen

16½"

20"

6½" head space

inner barn floor

sweep-out space at either end

cement blocks

floor of goat pen

of hay. Since there is more latitude for the goats to swing their heads back and forth, there is less chance of an unwary goat being pinned against the slats by an aggressive pen-mate. The closely spaced slats also prevent young kids from climbing into the manger and soiling the hay. A manger 15 feet long will accommodate eight goats. We nail a short chain and snap lock to the framing studs every 22 inches to keep the goats in their places at milking/feeding time. (Feeding time from their point of view, milking from ours!)

We use a different sort of manger for the sheep—a rack, really—made of 1½-inch spindles set at an angle in two 9-foot-long 2 by 4s. The whole assembly is nailed to the wall of their pen. The rack was part of a longer manger salvaged from the old barn. We cut it down and reset it at convenient sheep height—2½ feet from the floor. Under the rack, a small shelf holds a salt block.

We also built outside mangers for the buck and doe yards where we can feed coarse brush, corn fodder, soybean stalks and such, brought in from the fields. These extra mangers provide an alternative feeding station for shy goats who may be chased away from the indoor manger by more aggressive members of the herd. The roof helps to protect the hay from rain, and the goats from the sun, as well as to stabilize the whole arrangement. The slats on the goats' side of the manger, you will

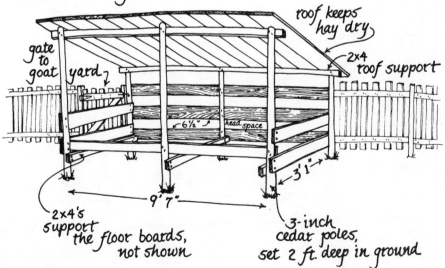

Outdoor Manger

roof keeps hay dry

gate to goat yard

2x4 roof support

6½" head space

2x4's support the floor boards, not shown

9' 7"

3' 1"

3-inch cedar poles, set 2 ft. deep in ground

119

notice, extend high enough to discourage them from climbing into the manger. None of them has ever climbed or jumped out through the manger. (But a stray gypsy goat once joined our herd by somehow jumping *into* the loafing yard from the outside, through that rather narrow opening!)

The framework of the outside manger consists of six cedar posts, cut on the farm, set in the ground to a depth of 2 feet. The posts are in line with the fencing posts around the goat yard and were set at the same time. A piece of scrap 2 by 4, nailed 10 inches above the ground, connects each pair of posts. The floor of the 3-foot-wide manger, made of 1-inch lumber, is nailed to the supporting 2-by-4 crosspieces. The sides are nailed to the posts. The tops of the posts are bevelled to support the roof. The superstructure of the manger is braced, and the roof further supported, by two 2 by 4s nailed to the posts, flush with the top, and running the width of the manger, front and back.

The arrangement is simple and rather crudely put together, but it has lasted well and has made our goat feeding program more versatile.

The Pig Palace

Building the right kind of quarters for your pigs can save you a lot of time and trouble in raising them. Pigs need:

• Some protection from very cold weather.

• Shade in summer—essential since their skin has no cooling sweat glands.

• *Strong* fencing.

• Securely mounted feed trough. Stepping in the trough and rooting under it are normal pig games.

• Sufficient space to permit them to leave their droppings at some distance from their eating and sleeping area.

We raise two pigs each year to supply our family with meat. For the first few years, we kept the pigs on the ground from March to October in a scrap-wood A-frame surrounded by two strands of electric wire fencing.

There were several problems with this arrangement, though:

1. The A-frame sheltered the pigs fairly well from the **sun**, but not from the cold. It was too tall and too open.

2. The nitrogen-rich droppings were lost to us when we did not confine the pigs on rotated vegetable garden ground, because the pigs rooted them into the muck.

3. In rooting the soil, the pigs threw up a mound of dirt around the edge of their electric-wired enclosure that often shorted out the electric wire.

4. Weeds growing close to the electric wire required frequent scything so that they wouldn't touch the wire and interrupt the flow of current.

For our fifth year of pig raising, we decided to build a compact, sturdy pig house that would shelter our pigs in all weather. The house, with its low ceiling, traps body heat; in cold weather the pigs keep each other warm. The low end of the sloping roof faces west, presenting less area to bear the brunt of westerly wind and to absorb heat rays from the strong western summer sun. The doorway is on the east side, and above it the high end of the roof overhangs to form a porch. Shade cast by the roof overhang in the afternoon sun will provide a cool spot for the growing pigs even in midsummer.

1x5 slats

guillotine door

Overall layout of Pig Palace

Platform

locust 2x4's

feed trough

overhang

entrance

House

2x4 stake: sunk in ground; protrudes 18 inches above ground to stabilize house (both sides)

Next to the pighouse, we built a platform of one-inch oak planks, rough-sawn on a neighbor's sawmill from a tree Mike had cut in our woods. The platform rests on a foundation of concrete blocks spaced on 30-inch centers, topped with 4-by-4 joists. The platform is butted close to the house, but it is erected separately. Each structure stands independently on its own foundation. Around the perimeter of the platform, we nailed a hog-tight fence of 1-by-6 boards supported by 2-by-4 locust posts. We secured the iron feed trough in position with pieces of scrap wood, nailed to the platform so that the pigs couldn't play shuffleboard with their feed dish.

This kind of setup is by no means the only way to raise pigs. Barn confinement on concrete, open range in pasture or garden and small fenced plots are other options used successfully by many homesteaders. Our arrangement, though, is the result of several years of experience and trial and error, and it has been most satisfactory for us.

The pigs do leave their manure at the far end of the enclosure, at the greatest possible distance from their eating area. The rectangular shape of the platform makes it easier for the pigs to cooperate. A square platform would crowd the clean and contaminated areas too close, unless it was a large area. If you should build this kind of housing for your pigs, you will want to remember to give them a shovelful of earth from time to time so that they can root in it for natural antibiotics. We rake out the droppings periodically and add them to the compost pile.

As you can see in the diagram, we positioned ten concrete blocks in two rows 5½ feet apart, to form the foundation for the platform "patio." If your ground is not perfectly flat, you may need to dig away a bit of earth so that the tops of the blocks will be level. It's also possible, on the other hand, that, if you are using scrap wood, your 4-by-4 joists may vary in thickness. If that is the case, you can even things out by placing the blocks at slightly different levels, as necessary, to compensate for the post variations. This is easier to do if you start at the high end of your ground (if any) and work down.

First concrete blocks, then joists, next the platform flooring. As mentioned above, we used rough-cut random-width oak planks for strength and durability. Notice how we nailed the planks to the joists. Why? The first method forms a much stronger surface. As you can see, the uniform line of butted planks in the second sketch would create a weak point, almost a hinge, in the platform. The structure of alternated board lengths is much stronger. Of course, we could have used

A pig's-eye view of dinner coming. The roof overhang on the hog house provides welcome shade in summer.

The pig palace. The board-flap that keeps the geese out of the pigs' feed is raised here—on hinges. Note roof overhang for shade.

Mike Bubel

T. L. Gettings

Dinner time for the pigs. The hinged flap extending the full length of the hog trough keeps the ducks from helping themselves to the pigs' feed.

Mike Bubel

Pig palace looking toward barn. The extra slat kept the pigs in when they were very small.

T. L. Gettings

planks that would extend the whole way across the platform without seams, if we had had some. But we didn't, and we suspect that many of you won't, either. The alternative is to make sound use of what *is* available. Using alternating board lengths like this saves on lumber without adversely affecting the quality of the structure. A wide board bends less than a narrow one, so if you are using boards of random width, place the widest ones where you expect stress to be greatest—in our case here, in the center of the platform.

In nailing the planks, we didn't worry about butting their long edges too tightly together, since we wanted to allow for drainage and air circulation. In this case, a perfect fit between boards is not an ideal to strive for. We left a ½- to ¾-inch space between the boards— large enough to allow air circulation but not so wide that the pigs would catch their feet in the gap. Boards on a level surface that butt together perfectly edge to edge won't dry readily after rain and may rot sooner than those nailed with slight gaps. The butt ends of the planks, of course, should fit together as well as possible to avoid forming pockets that would retain standing water on the joists.

We also tried to avoid laying planks with knots and holes exposed on the top side, in order to prevent rot from standing rain and/or expanding and cracking of the wood by moisture freezing. Always turn the soundest side of the plank facing up.

After constructing the platform, we started on the house, which was set on a foundation of four concrete blocks, topped by two 4-by-4 posts. Construction steps followed this order:

1. We first made the floor by nailing boards to 2-by-4 joists with a double 2 by 4 in the center for added strength.

2. Then we nailed the siding boards to an offset 2 by 4 (see diagram).

3. Next, we set the walls in place and nailed a strip of scrap wood between them to keep them in position while we nailed the walls to the 2-by-4 joists.

4. Nail boards across back and front horizontally, leaving space for the doorway. Be sure to avoid ending at the top with a narrow strip of wood which would form a weak edge. If your lumber is all the same size, plan the height of your structure to fit the wood on hand. Before nailing the last piece of wood siding to the back of the pig house, we measured and marked the size it should be and ripped it with a circular saw.

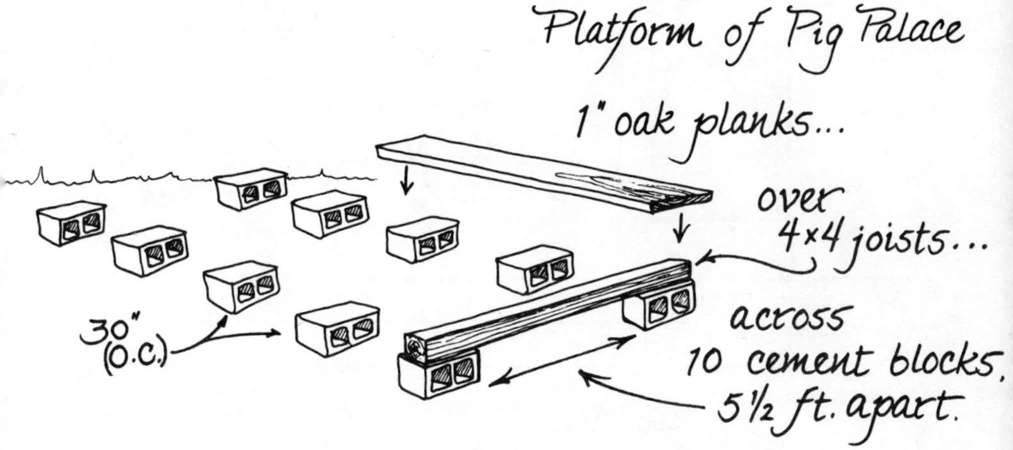

Platform of Pig Palace

1" oak planks...

over
4×4 joists...

across
10 cement blocks,
5½ ft. apart.

30"
(O.C.)

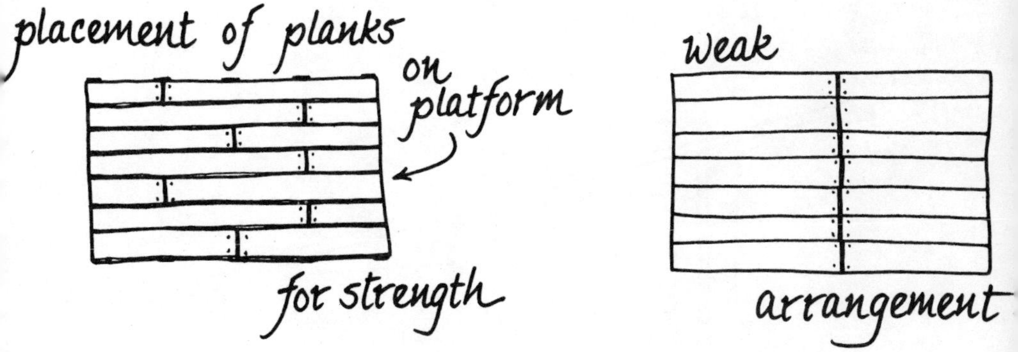

placement of planks
on
platform

weak

for strength

arrangement

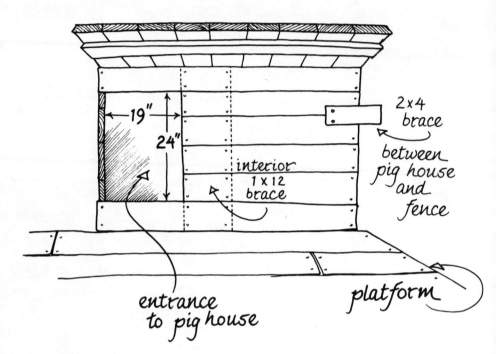

19"

24"

interior
1 x 12
brace

2x4
brace

*between
pig house
and
fence*

entrance
to pig house

platform

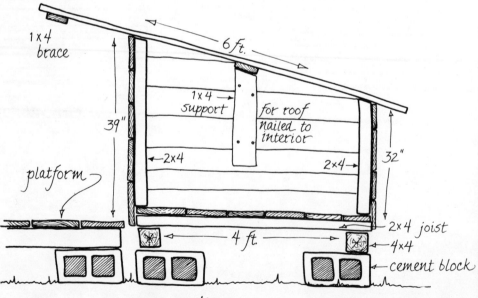

1 x 4
brace

6 ft.

1x4
support

for roof
nailed to
interior

39"

2x4

2x4

32"

platform

2x4 joist

4 ft.

4x4

cement block

cross section

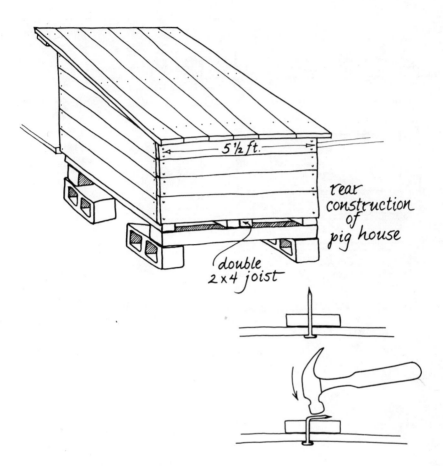

rear
construction
of
pig house

5½ ft.

double
2 x 4 joist

5. Nail on roof boards, allowing overhang for shade.

6. Nail brace at edge of roof overhang and also in middle of roof, from underneath. Flatten protruding nails for safety.

7. To further support the roof, nail a vertical brace on each side wall butting with roof brace (see diagram).

8. Nail on roll roofing, using roofing nails. Be sure top layer overlaps bottom layer!

9. For extra weatherproofing in severe climates, roll roofing may be nailed across the windward-side wall of the pig house, overlapped shingle-style.

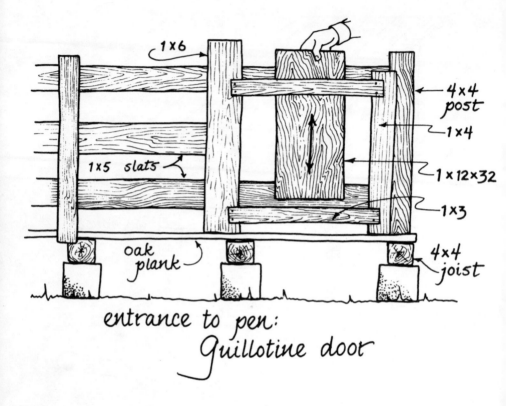

1×6

4×4
post

1×4

1×5 slats

1×12×32

1×3

oak
plank

4×4
joist

entrance to pen:
guillotine door

space for
sliding board

1×5 slat

4×4
post

1×6

1×3

1×4

– view
from top –

rasped edges

1x5 slats

iron feed trough

short cleats prevent trough from shifting

1x11 *flap board*

bevelled 2x3

1x5 slat

bevelled-2x3 trough brace

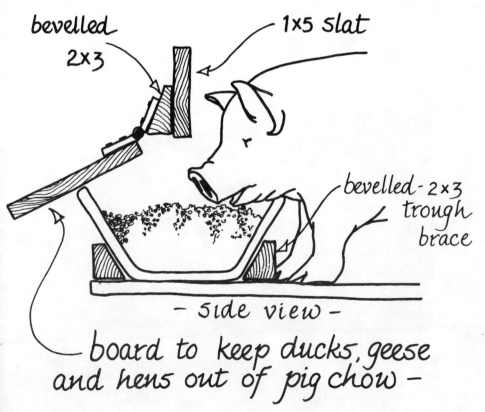

- side view -

board to keep ducks, geese and hens out of pig chow -

With the house completed, we enclosed the platform with a sturdy fence supported by 2-by-4 locust posts, cut on our place and squared off by our friendly neighborhood sawmill operator. The posts are pounded about 15 inches into the ground. The fence boards are 1 by 5s of locust and oak. Nailing the boards on the inside of the post makes the fence more resistant to outward pressure from the pigs. Notice how the fence ties the posts together and the platform supports the posts too. We placed a single strut, a 1 by 3, across the center of the enclosure, between posts, to further stabilize the fence. The guillotine-type gate is simply a 1-by-12 oak plank that fits in a slot in the fence and rests on a 1-by-3 stop nailed to the platform.

We took care to rasp off the top edges of the posts to eliminate "furred" or splintered edges that might catch and hold rain and encourage rot.

With our new pig quarters, we find it possible to buy pigs earlier in the season, since the house protects them well from the cold. We can keep a pig later in the fall, too, to make use of late garden and canning leftovers. The pigs have shade from the sun and a stabilized trough. And we have the bonus of rich manure that we can spread on the garden rather than leaving it to sink into the muck of a permanent pig plot.

T. L. Gettings

Mike operating guillotine loading door on pig palace. It's good the pigs don't know that board can be raised to leave an open space! Note manure/bedding at end of fenced area farthest from feed trough. Construction of platform—oak planks supported by 4x4s resting on concrete blocks—is shown here.

Animal Transport Crate

Any homesteader who keeps a few animals larger than rabbits will at least occasionally need a way of transporting them from auction to farm, homestead to butcher, or barn to breeding sire. You can't very well carry two 225-pound pigs in the backseat of your car or the cab or the unprotected bed of your pickup truck. Even if you do your own butchering, there will be times when you will want to pick up or deliver animals.

The solution we've worked out for ourselves assumes the ready use of a truck—either one that you own or one you've borrowed. The truck we started out with, an ancient third-hand Chevy with a home-made top mounted on the bed, was easy to adapt for carrying animals; we closed the tailgate and fastened on an expanding lattice gate (the kind used to protect toddlers) to cover the rest of the back opening. This wouldn't have worked for transporting a bull, but then we never had a bull. We carried sheep, pigs and goats in the back of Homer, the truck, and never lost one.

The inevitable day came, though, when Homer had to be replaced. The sides of our new truck bed are too low to confine any active animal. We needed a travel crate that would keep the animals confined, secure and comfortable on their trip. The crate should fit well into the truck bed and be readily mounted and removed. It should provide easy access for the animals to enter, but no weak spots where may might push out.

Mike Bubel

Nancy helps Evie-the-Goat up the ramp into the animal transport crate positioned on the back of the pickup.

With the passenger safely on board, she slides the closing slats into position on the back of the crate.

Mike Bubel

She then fastens the latch at the end of each closing slat.

Mike Bubel

The crate we built is made of unplaned 2 by 3s and 1 by 3s from knocked-down snowmobile crates. Essentially it is a rectangular framework with cross braces on the ceiling, and no floor. The opening, through which the animals are loaded and unloaded, is closed over with removable 1-by-3 slats held in place by small blocks of wood nailed to the frame so that they rotate to fit into notches in the ends of the slats.

To make loading easier, we use a ramp made of an oak plank with 1-inch sticks nailed on at 10-inch intervals to give the animals better footing. The ramp fits between the crate and the side of the truck. If it is necessary to transport animals in cold or stormy weather, we tie tarps over the top and sides of the crate to shield our passengers from wind. The crate will hold three grown sheep, three 200-pound pigs, eight to ten kids, or four to five adult goats. We have used it to take sheep, pigs and goats to the butcher, to pick up animals we wanted to buy, to take doe goats to registered bucks for breeding and to transport our milking does to the farm of friends who would milk them while we took a family trip. The crate has even done double duty on occasion, as on the November day when I took the sheep to the butcher and returned home with the enclosed space piled high with bags of leaves collected in town.

The sketch shows the dimensions of our crate, made to fit between the wheel wells in the bed of a 1975 Datsun pickup with a 6-foot bed.

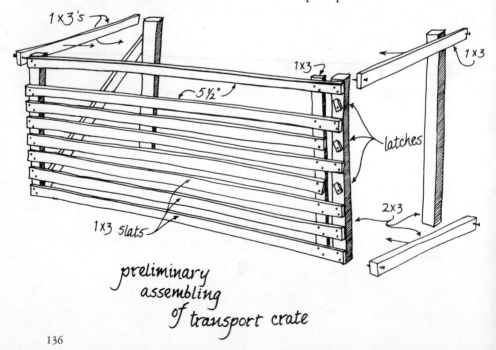

1 x 3's

1 x 3

1 x 3

5½"

latches

1 x 3 slats

2 x 3

preliminary
assembling
of transport crate

top-bracing of crate

cab end ⟶

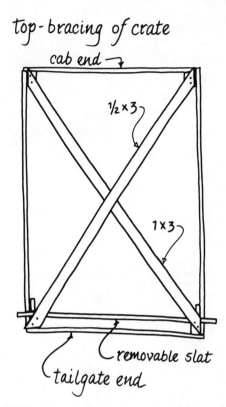

½ × 3⟍

1 × 3⟍

⟍*removable slat*

⟍*tailgate end*

If your truck bed is wider or longer than ours, simply adjust the length of your side or end boards to fit. For a crate to fit an 8-foot truck bed, you might want to add an extra sidebrace.

Here's how we made the transport crate:

1. Assemble the sides first: Nail eight 1-by-3 slats to three 2 by 3s to form a grid, leaving a 1-inch space between the seven bottom slats and a 5½-inch space between the top two slats. Nail an extra vertical 1 by 3 on the tailgate end of the side grid, leaving a 1¼-inch space between the 1 by 3 and the 2 by 3 on the end. These 1¼-inch spaces will admit the three removable 1-by-3 slats that close over the end of the crate. Make another side grid, but not exactly like the first one: the extra 1 by 3 should be on the opposite end, so that your two crate sides are mirror images of each other. Nail three "latches" of one-inch scrap wood, sanded down a bit so that they will fit into the one-inch grooves, to the corner 2 by 3 at points 5 inches, 13½ inches, and 21 inches from the top of the crate.

2. Ends: Join the two side pieces by nailing a 38-inch 2 by 3 to each of the four upright corner 2 by 3s at the bottom, and a 1 by 3 at the top. Nail a diagonal 1-by-3 brace to the two corner 2 by 3s on the narrow end of the crate that will be nearest the cab of the truck. At the outer, tail-gate end of the crate, nail two ½-by-3-inch braces at approximately 40-degree angles from the top 1 by 3 to the corner 2 by 3. These braces are nailed outside the corner 2 by 3s at their lower ends, and inside the top 1 by 3s at their upper ends.

slat-latches:

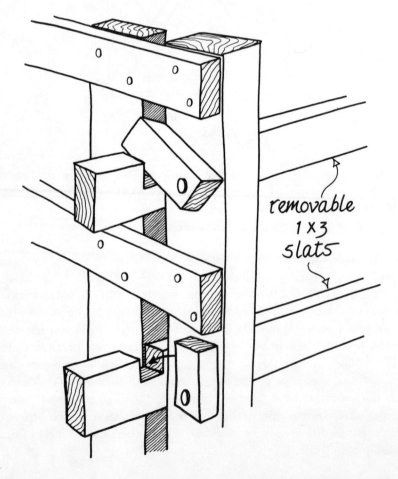

removable 1 X 3 slats

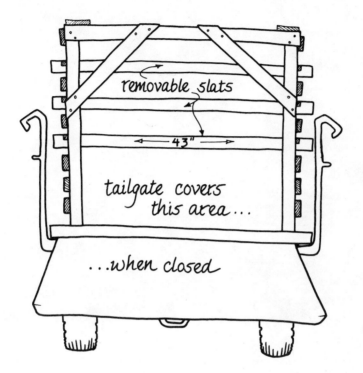

removable slats

43"

tailgate covers
this area...

...when closed

3. Top: Nail two diagonal pieces: a 1 by 3 from corner to corner, and on top of it a ½ by 3, joining the opposite corners and the 1 by 3. This cross brace keeps animals from climbing out, stabilizes the crate and provides support for a tarp when it is necessary to use one.

4. Closing slats: Cut three 1 by 3s 43 inches long. Cut a 1-inch deep, 1-inch wide groove in each slat, 3 inches from one end.

When the animal is on the truck and the tailgate is closed, the slats may be quickly latched in place to block the remaining open space in the end of the crate. If you find that your slats do not fit equally well in each space, number them with a marking crayon or wood-burning pen to indicate the order in which they should be inserted for the best fit.

Store the crate under cover when not in use, unless you've made it of cedar, locust or other weather-resistant wood.

During the summer, you can use the crate as a drying rack for dehydrating garden fruits and vegetables—just improvise screen supports between the side slats and set a drying screen on the top.

Mike Bubel

Rolling on: Evie can look out the rear of the crate to see where she's been.

Feed Bin

Storage of feed grain is a basic necessity on any homestead, large or small. Trash cans may be used to store feed safely in small amounts, but with all that empty space between the round forms, using more than one or two cans wastes floor space. Not only that, but when you have eight or ten feed pans to fill, juggling them between trash can lids can be inconvenient to say the least. We expect a lot of our feed bins, you see. They must:

1. Provide clean, dry, dust-free storage for the variety of grains and pellets consumed by our mixed population of animals.

2. Protect the grain from consumption and contamination by rats and mice.

3. Give us a working surface for doling out and custom-mixing grains.

4. Be easy to reach into and to clean.

5. Allow us to order feed in bulk from the mill, thus saving us time and gas. The feed mill truck brings our order on its regular rounds. When we stored grain in trash cans, we seldom had room for enough grain to qualify for the 500-pound minimum necessary for free delivery.

6. Have enough compartments to separate the different grains and pellets we use in the course of the year:

oats	laying mash
corn—whole and cracked	hog feed
bran	growing mash
goats' fitting ration	dog food

When building the barn, we left an "L" of wall space on the north barn wall and the west wall of the workshop for the feed bins— close to the barn door for ease in delivering feed, and adjacent to the sink and milking area. We decided against making the bins built-in to the building, electing instead to build two freestanding bins that could be easily shifted or repaired if necessary.

The bins are constructed of 1-by-2 and 2-by-4 studs and 1-inch tongue-and-groove siding with 1-inch plywood dividers. One bin contains five 15-by-28-by-23-inch compartments, the other has four. The bin lids are 26 inches wide, with a 13½-inch front section hinged to allow access. The hinged part of the lids folds back flat to provide a

T. L. Gettings

Bins are raised on blocks to discourage rats.

work surface. Then, if any grain is spilled, it is tipped back into the bin when the flap is closed. The slanted front of the bin allows us easier access to feed when the level is low.

We set the bins on concrete blocks to eliminate narrow, low floor spaces where rodents might hide and nest. We also tacked flexible aluminum plates (purchased from a newspaper printer) to the back and underside of the bins to keep them safe from gnawing rodents.

Construction of the feed bin went as follows:

1. We made the floor by nailing 1-inch tongue-and-groove to two 2 by 4s. The 2 by 4s run the length of the bins, making it possible for

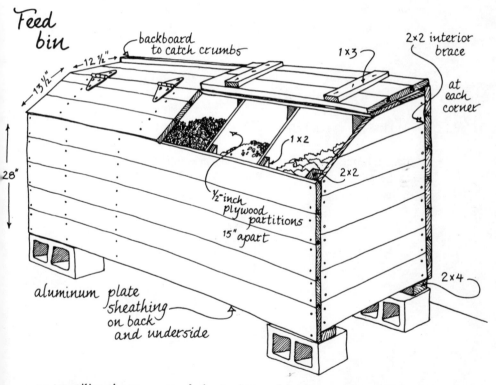

us to utilize the many good short pieces of tongue-and-groove that we had on hand to run the width, rather than the length, of the feed box.

Then we:

2. Nailed 1-inch tongue-and-groove to two 2-by-2 corner braces for the front panel and did the same for the back panel. The lowest board

on the front panel extends 1½ inches below its corner brace; thus it overlaps the floor when fitted in place.

3. Nailed braces every 15 inches (O.C.) to support front and back panels and provide attachment for bin dividers.

4. Nailed tongue-and-groove boards between the front and back panels to form the sides of the bin. Whenever using tongue-and-groove vertically, we try to have the tongue facing up and the groove on top,— a woodbutcher's ounce of prevention that helps the wood to last longer. As you can see from the sketch, placing the grooved board underneath the tongue forms a pocket that may collect moisture. As you remember, wood lasts for ages when kept dry, but soon rots if subjected to continuous dampness.

5. Cut bin dividers to fit the interior of the bin and nailed them to the 1-by-2 braces of the front and back panels.

6. Nailed the rigid back half of the lid to the top of the bin.

7. Made the hinged part of the lid by nailing tongue-and-groove siding to two 1-by-3-inch crosspieces. The hinged lid is attached to the rigid lid with five-inch hinges.

8. Tacked aluminum plates to the back and underside of the bin.

Barn Gates

Sooner or later, you'll need a few good gates around your homestead. While a casually erected fence will serve its purpose for a year or so, and a rickety woodshed will last a surprising number of years, a poorly made gate will be a headache from the start.

Gates are subject to daily stress, with the opening and closing necessary for barn chores, as well as the pushing and rubbing by animals, to whom a gate is often a great challenge. A gate should swing freely and easily on its hinges. The hinges themselves should be strong enough to bear the load of the gate. The gate should provide easy access to the pen, yard or whatever for the homesteader, but be securely latched in such a way that the animals confined behind it cannot reach over or turn it to trip the latch. The gateway opening should be wide enough to admit any garden carts or other equipment that you might want to take through it.

The choice of a latch should be one of your first considerations, since it will determine the placement of your gate in relation to its supporting posts. We favor the self-closing latch illustrated in the photo. It is widely available in hardware and farm supply stores. If you want to use this latch inside a pen, as for a kid creep or maternity pen walled off from a larger enclosure, you will find that the goats soon learn to open the latch. Foil them by fastening a snap lock through the hole to block the tripping mechanism. Usually, though, this latch is used on

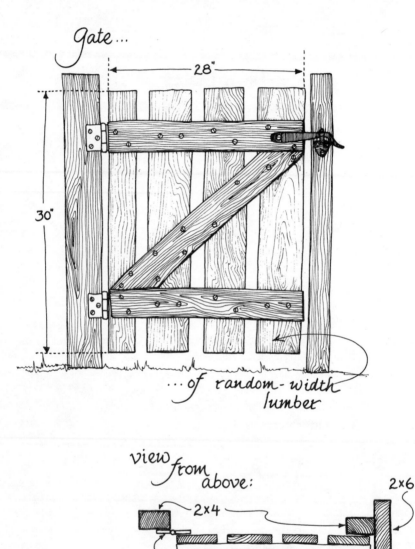

gate...

28"

30"

...of random-width lumber

view from above:

2x4

2x6

hinge

latch

the outside of a gate, positioned far enough from the top of the gate so that agile animals cannot reach over and open it. Or you may want to improvise a sliding wood latch, or use a hook and eye, sliding bolt or thumb latch.

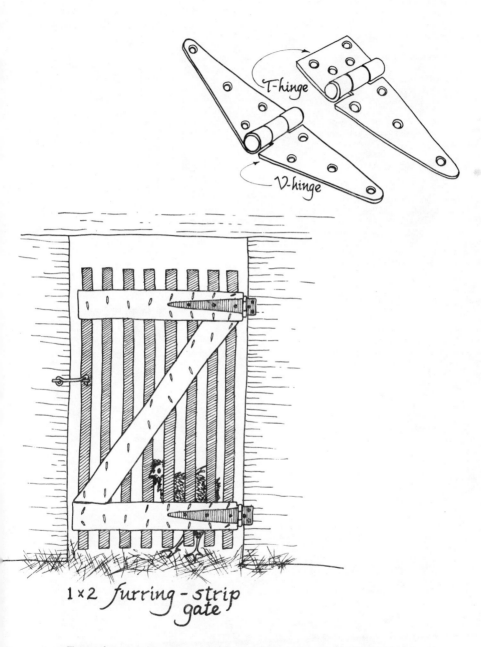

1×2 *furring-strip gate*

For a heavy gate, you might consider using a T-hinge if there is enough solid gate surface to attach the long arm of the hinge.

Hinges, as you no doubt know, should *always* be screwed in, never nailed. Use a screw long enough to penetrate most of the board, just

147

This self-closing latch is our favorite goat-proof gate closure. The animals soon learn to trip the latch if it's on *their* side of the gate, though.

Mike Bubel

An old hook-and-eye gate latch.

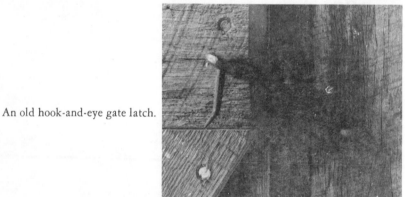

Mike Bubel

Mike Bubel

An easy way to hold a fence or door flap open or closed: a short length of chain hooked onto a nail on the flap and a nail on the fence.

Mike Bubel

The gate to our hen pen is made of narrowly spaced furring strips. Note that cutout strip (at upper left) permits us to trip the latch from inside the pen. We tried a string for awhile but find this easier—no friction.

Mike Bubel

As you can see, there are no footholds for adventurous climbing animals on this typical barn gate.

short of puncturing it through. Many packaged hinge sets provide inadequate short screws. We'd recommend using good long screws to put together your busy barn gate.

We've made gates out of old screen doors, furring strips, scrap 1 by 4s and salvaged barn stable doors. The screen-door gate, reinforced with lath strips, was our temporary solution to a short-term situation. It closed off a small yard next to our temporary goat pen while we were building the barn. The furring strip gate gives floor-to-ceiling coverage for our hens, admitting air and light. The strips are too closely spaced to allow the hens to squeeze through.

We cut down an old stable door to make a gate for the sheep pen. All it required was careful measuring and application of hinges.

Our favorite gate is the classic one illustrated in the photo. For this we used weathered but sound old 1-inch boards, old hinges and new hardware. Notice that the brace and crosspieces are on the outside of the gate so that the animals can't climb on it. The vertical boards are placed close together for the same reason. All gate boards are screwed together, not nailed.

Begin by measuring the space between the posts that will support your gate. If the top and bottom measurements are too far out of line, you'll have to straighten your post, or the gate won't swing! This is less likely to be a problem in a building than in a fence. Allow about ½ inch of clearance on each side of the gate to give it room to swing. (Your gate frame should measure 1 inch less than the opening between its supporting posts.)

Measure and cut the vertical boards for the gate. Make the gate long enough to keep the animals from jumping over or crawling under. Cut the crosspieces that fasten the vertical boards together at top and bottom. Assemble the gate on a flat surface, mark the correct placement of the upper and lower horizontal crosspieces, and drive screws to fasten each vertical board to the crosspieces, keeping all angles square. Then place a 1-by-6 brace across the assembled gate, marking cutting lines. Cut the brace to fit between the crosspieces and screw it into place. Screw the hinges on. (Drill a starting hole first.) A gate that is over 5 feet high or 3 feet wide needs three hinges. Attach the gate portion of the latch. Next prop the gate in position or have a helper steady it while you fasten the remaining hinge flap to the supporting post and then complete the latch closure on the opposite side.

Perhaps we find these barn gates so satisfying because they display nicely grained old wood, do their job reliably, and have an honest, functional, no-nonsense design that pleases us. At any rate, they serve to keep the animals in what we think of as their place; we are at the same time always conscious that their idea of their place has more to do with their desire to prune our grape vines and sample our bean crop. We sympathize, but we latch the gate.

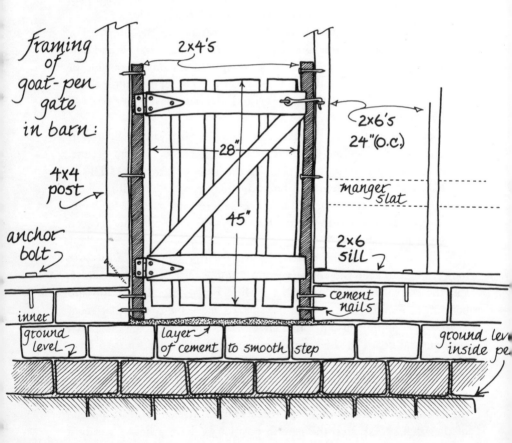

framing
of
goat-pen
gate
in barn:

2x4's

2x6's
24"(o.c.)

manger slat

4x4
post

28"

45"

2x6
sill

anchor
bolt

cement
nails

inner
ground
level

layer
of cement

to smooth

step

ground level
inside pe...

Equipment Shed

Our equipment shed is a more primitive construction than the barn, but nonetheless sturdy. We needed shelter for our ancient tractor to extend its usefulness through at least a few more winters. We also had a new truck that we wanted to protect. In addition, we had accumulated a modest collection of useful outdoor machinery: a rototiller, a hand-pushed power sicklebar mower, bicycles, garden carts and such—things that should be stored under cover. Some of them were in the barn, but they were in the way there. Furthermore, we had on hand a large stack of heavy 8-by-8-inch and 10-by-12-inch handhewn beams saved from the salvaged barn. Storage in the open was not improving them any, and they were too good to waste. The obvious solution, to both of these concerns, was to build a structure that would utilize our good wood to advantage without cutting it up too much, and shelter our old but useful equipment.

The building had to be tall enough to permit us to drive the tractor into it without getting scalped, and wide enough to leave room for bikes to lean on its interior partition. The other important consideration was the approach. The entrance to the building should be easily accessible from the lane so that we wouldn't have a long driveway to shovel in snow or muck through in mud. The structure should not block our view of the mountain, the woods behind our house, our fields or our neighbor's farm—all vistas that we enjoy taking in as we work around the house and fields. On the other hand, the building should make practical use of the century-old beams in a way that would allow us to continue to appreciate their interesting texture and imposing solidity.

What evolved was a three-sided log-cabin-type structure, open to the south and facing the driveway, near the lane. To gain more storage space, we built in a loft, giving us a fine place to keep board lumber, bushel baskets, tarps and other homestead necessities, as well as to store nuts, and—until heavy frost—apples.

The log shed is situated on ground that drains well. Since there is only one interior wall, and no floor, plastering, plumbing or other fine work to be ruined by slight changes in level due to frost heaving, we used simple footings of concrete blocks, set in the ground in pairs at 10-to-12-foot intervals. The blocks are surrounded by concrete to prevent water from soaking into the ground immediately around them and causing subsidence or heaving from frost action.

The first step, after determining the dimensions and position of the shed, was to use pickax and shovel to dig the holes for the concrete

Log Shed

five
3×6 planks
form
loft

24 ft.

rafter brace

2×6 rafter - 14 each side

6×6 post

4×4 brace

2×10 plank

spliced logs

21 ft.

block footings, using a level to position the blocks and sighting from one to another to assure even height. In placing the blocks in their excavations, it is important to put them on firm soil. If a hole must be filled in slightly to bring the height of the block up to that of other blocks, then any soft soil on the bottom of the hole should be very firmly tamped in place. Otherwise the block will soon settle deeper into the hole.

Once the concrete block footings were in place, we began to position the first course of beams. Mike and Greg dragged the beams, one at a time, from their storage pile to the building site, using a tractor and chain. Some were quite rough—half logs, really—rounded on two sides and squared off with an adze on the other sides. These pieces had been the joists under the heavy planks that formed the tractor-parking floor in the barn we had torn down. Dealing with wood of such massive bulk gives one a new appreciation of what *heavy* is. The beams we were using ranged from an estimated 400 pounds to 1,000 pounds.

Mike Bubel

Side front view of the log shed. The tractor is parked out of sight behind the bikes on left side. Facing planks of oak cover cut edges of the logs facing the driveway. We attached an old rain gutter to the west side of the shed to direct rainwater away from the building's foundation.

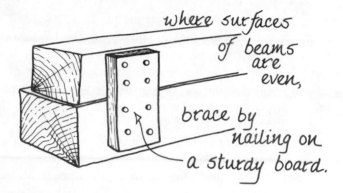

where surfaces
of beams
are
even,

brace by
nailing on
a sturdy board.

triangular hole
chipped
into beam...

...for stronger
spike-
hold

details of log joinery:

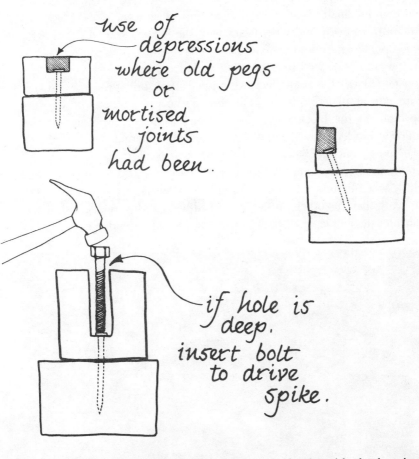

use of depressions where old pegs or mortised joints had been.

if hole is deep, insert bolt to drive spike.

Naturally, the sensible thing to do was to begin with the heaviest logs, so that we wouldn't have to lift them so far. How do you begin on a heavy job like that? The answer, we all learned, is an inch at a time, then a foot at a time. Do the work in stages. Getting one course of logs in place took considerable effort and strategy, but each course added a visible 8 to 10 inches to the height of the building—a large and immediate difference that spurred us on.

When delivering the beams to the construction site, Mike and Greg dragged them as close as possible to the wall where we wanted them.

We then made use of the good old lever and fulcrum technique to raise the logs into position. Place the end of the log on a small block of wood, either by raising that end with a crowbar or, if the log is very heavy, by rolling it over onto the block. With the log thus elevated, even if only an inch or so above the ground, we positioned a concrete block and a small block of wood next to it. Using the wood block as a fulcrum, we pried under the beam with the lever—a crowbar or sturdy wood pole—and raised one end of the log to rest on the concrete block. In the same way, we lifted the other end of the beam to rest on another concrete block. Or, sometimes, we slipped a pole under the low end and, with one or two people on each end of the pole, raised the log into position on the block. We then had a heavy beam resting on two concrete blocks situated parallel to its eventual permanent position on two more concrete blocks, as the first course of the shed wall. To jimmy the log over onto its final resting place, we used another concrete block as a fulcrum, a tough wood pole as a lever, and we set over first one end, then the other. When it worked well, and it usually did, it was ridiculously simple, even though the task looked formidable.

T. L. Gettings

Mike inspects the east wall of the log shed. Note that the longest, heaviest logs were set in place first.

Chipping away a triangular section of log made it possible for us to sink a spike that would attach the upper log firmly to the one below it.

Mike Bubel

Detail of one front edge of the log shed showing concrete block footings and oak facing board.

Mike Bubel

Succeeding courses of logs were added, using the same principles mentioned here and in Chapter Four. The laws of physics don't change. There is a dependable order in the earth. You can count on it—even when you're five courses up and the logs aren't getting much lighter. When you begin to get an inkling of how things work, you can sense a trustworthiness at the root of matter, and the world under your feet seems at once more solid and more mysterious.

So the log-beams were piled up, levered and coaxed into position. We reserved the shorter, slightly thinner (6 by 8 inch) beams for building up the top courses to save effort in lifting.

We didn't just pile up big Lincoln logs, though. Each course was tied in to the beams below it by interlocking the corners and spiking the other logs that didn't extend to the corner.

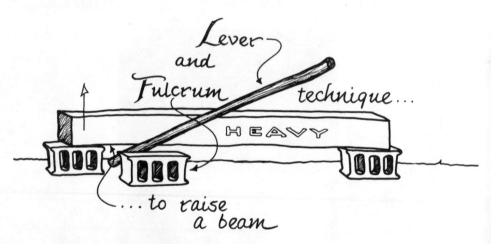

Lever and Fulcrum technique... ...to raise a beam

HEAVY

Beams to be joined, either at the corners or in the middle of the wall, were mortised as shown in the diagram. This method of joinery made it possible to drive two spikes into the end of log A to connect it to log C below it, and then to connect log B to A with two more spikes. The joinery we used was not finely detailed. The logs are rough, the ends sometimes uneven, and the finishing inelegant but straightforward. It would probably be too rough for a house, but the building is sturdy and solid and it serves its purpose without pretending to be what it is not.

The beams were additionally secured to each other by means of toenailing. On some heavy beams, Mike used a hatchet to chip away a triangular wedge of wood to allow deeper sinking of the spike.

mortised logs

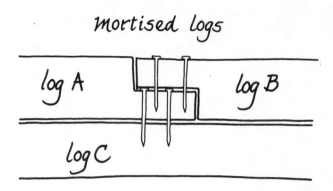

The 21-by-24-foot building is braced by the interlocking corners and also by the plate and pediment across the open end and the loft. Three vertical 2-by-10 planks nailed over the cut ends of the logs on the open side add stability and a smoother appearance.

Four double 2 by 6s fit into the next-to-the-last course of beams, extending from the west wall to the interior wall, and from the interior wall to the east wall. These joists support the loft planks laid across them. On the top course of the interior wall we toenailed three 6-by-6 posts, each braced with 4 by 4s, to support a 6-by-8-inch ridgepole, which also rests on the pediment of the north and south ends of the shed. We spaced new 2-by-6 fir rafters at 2-foot intervals, resting on the top course of beams and butting the ridgepole. For furring strips, we used lengths of 1-inch tongue-and-groove siding, cut to 4-inch widths, and then we topped the building with a corrugated aluminum roof.

Once we had the roof on, we moved in our tractor, truck, garden implements and bikes. We spread walnuts to dry on screens in the loft and stored apples there for several months. And our son discovered that the well-lit, open-air but protected shed makes a fine setting for his bike repair work.

As our complex of homestead buildings has grown, we've found that we needed a way of referring to them that would differentiate among them. The barn and the garage were obvious and easy, but what would we call *this* building—the log shed? "Equipment shed" is really too cumbersome a term. The problem appeared to be solved when we found ourselves calling the big new shed the "Homer Memorial"— after our first, fondly remembered, rattley but faithful (to the end, last summer) 1953 Chevy pickup, Homer.

Building a Homestead Barn

Perhaps it is just as well that there was no barn here on our farm, for we had a chance to plan and build a structure that would be a real homestead barn, custom designed for us and our animals. Mike pored over his graph-paper books every evening during the weeks before we moved to the farm, blocking out, changing, enlarging the plans for the barn. It was to be our first concern, our big thrust for the first summer on the farm. Although our previous building experience had been limited to the construction of two 6-by-8-foot sheds, we intended to build the barn ourselves, hiring help only when absolutely necessary. We started the last week of June with the excavation for the foundation, put the roof on over Labor Day weekend and finished nailing on the siding by October. Our family of four worked on the barn all day, almost every day, all summer.

In making the barn plan, Mike tailored the dimensions for most efficient utilization of our used lumber.

The layout of the barn allows for the Old MacDonald aspect of our homestead by providing small pens that can be used for different purposes. There is a pen and fenced run for the hens, a buck pen, a larger corner pen to house the sheep in bad weather which is also used for other purposes, as well as a spacious loafing area for the goats, complete with climbing platform, mangers and fenced yard with over-size outside manger for feeding coarse weeds and cornstalks. The main floor of the barn also includes a milking corner with stand, a sink, a

163

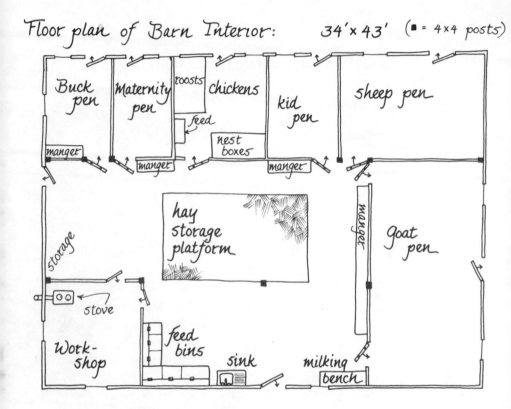

Floor plan of Barn Interior: 34' x 43'   (■ = 4x4 posts)

Buck pen | Maternity pen | toosts | chickens | kid pen | sheep pen
feed
nest boxes
manger | manger | manger

storage

hay storage platform

manger | goat pen

stove

Work-shop | feed bins | sink | milking bench

platform for hay storage, a feed-bin corner and a workshop. The work-shop is wired for power tools and heated by a small chunk stove. The barn floor is subsoil, laboriously hand-levelled and smoothed. We prefer it to concrete because it is less damp for the animals. Each pen has a door to the outside and at least one window. The goats like to look out the windows and, when penned next to the hens, seem to enjoy watching their antics.

The loft of the barn is floored by sturdy planking. There is room there for at least 800 bales of hay. We use part of the loft for storage and a section has been left unplanked so that we could easily toss hay down to the main floor. Access to the loft, so far, is by means of a folding stepladder which we mount easily when necessary, at most several times a week. Using a portable, rather than a fixed, ladder gives us more leeway in rearranging the loft layout to accommodate changing needs. A loading door from the loft opens out on the east side of the barn for convenient loading of hay.

In choosing the site for the barn, we had to juggle several important considerations.

1. To avoid even remotely possible contamination of our well by manure drainage, we located the barn downhill and at least 100 feet from the house.

2. We kept it close enough to the house, though, for ease in doing chores and for economy in laying underground electric and water lines.

3. We positioned the barn so that it wouldn't block the pleasant view from the kitchen, taking in fields, woods and mountains.

4. We tried to situate the barn so that it fit into its surroundings harmoniously. We wanted it to be a pleasing sight in its own right.

The barn is built into the gentle slope of the hill and shaded by black locust trees, about 120 feet from the house—a nice walk in any weather but not too far to carry the full milk bucket back up!

Once the site was chosen, the next step was to lay out the foundation lines with string, measuring very carefully and checking corner-to-corner measurements several times. We then sprinkled a thin line of lime all around, where the string was, to guide the backhoe operator in digging the trench for the foundation. The L-shaped interior trench provided for a concrete block barrier running around the side of each pen facing the inside of the barn. By doing this, we avoided putting wood partitions in direct contact with the ground and allowed for deep buildup of bedding with resulting composting effect.

The foundation trench we ordered was 2 feet deep at the shallowest spot, up to 4 feet deep where it cut into the hillside. This is well below frost line for our area. We used an old country trick to add stability to the foundation and save money on concrete fill: we tossed into the trench twenty wagonloads of stone taken from a pile at the edge of one of our fields. This meant that less concrete was needed to fill the trench. It also made a very strong foundation. Right after the trench was dug, and before we could fill it with rocks, a heavy rain filled the hole. When the water didn't drain out due to heavy clay subsoil—it just stayed there like a moat—we had to borrow a neighbor's sump pump to drain the

Surveying for the barn foundation.

Greg Bubel

The first course going up.   *Greg Bubel*

Putting the platform on the loft.

Nancy Bubel

The new barn with the ridgepole raised.

Greg Bubel

trench so we could get to work. You'd probably be wise to expect at
least one such proof of Murphy's Law, "If anything can go wrong, it
will," to occur on your construction project, too!

But we did get the trench drained and we somehow collected all
those rocks and tossed them in, then levelled them. Then we made forms
for the poured concrete foundation by positioning scrap boards at the
edge of the interior trench at the spots where the concrete would come
up near ground level.

The two weeks we spent on the trench and subsequent laying of
concrete blocks were the most exacting, tiring and discouraging of the
whole barn-building project. Nothing showed for the hours and hours
of time that we put into it, yet accuracy of measurement and careful

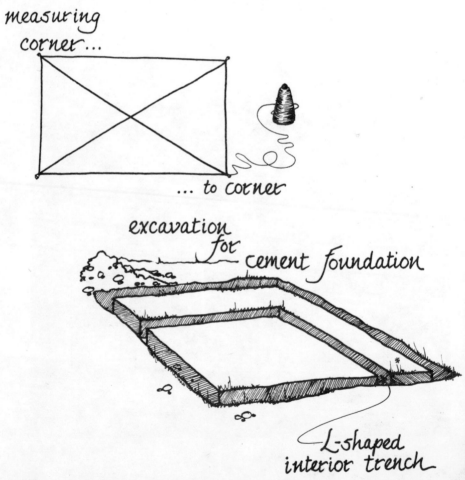

measuring corner...

... to corner

excavation for cement foundation

L-shaped interior trench

preparation were of the utmost importance. The whole success of the barn depended on what we were doing then, and underneath the grime and mud and blisters, we really knew that. So we slogged on.

The day came when we were ready for the concrete delivered by transit-mix truck right into the foundation trench. Allowing it to harden for a day was easy; we were glad for a rest, even if we did spend it pulling nails from old boards.

Mike had never done any concrete block work before, so he accepted, without hesitation, our good neighbor's offer of a half day's help in starting the job. While this book is no place for a course in laying blocks, you might like to know some of the rules for this kind of work that we learned while our neighbor worked with us.

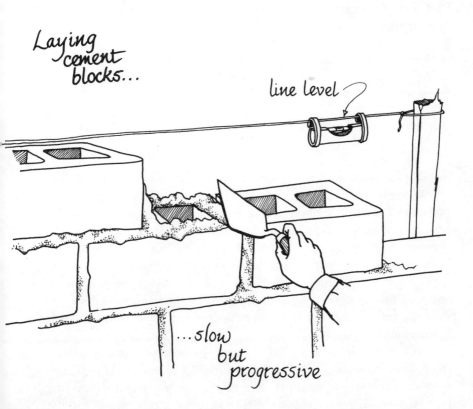

Laying cement blocks...

line level

...slow but progressive

1. There should be one-half inch of mortar between blocks.

2. Stretch a string to guide the edge of the concrete blocks as you lay them.

3. The proportions we used in our mortar were: two parts cement, six parts sand (1:3).

4. Slap mortar on sharply; this makes it go into the spaces and stick well.

5. Mortar should not be crumbly or runny.

6. Concrete blocks have one rough side; keep the rough side always either up or down, but be consistent. If laying smooth side on smooth, the bond won't be as good.

7. Check the level as you go and adjust uneven places by putting on more mortar.

8. You will need a pointed mason's hammer to break bricks.

9. Save enough corner blocks for corners and doorways.

10. Smooth out the last course to avoid hollows and level it accurately.

Laying block gradually evolved into a rhythm—not an easy one, but at least progressive. It was slow, though, and we were under pressure of time since heavy spring rains had delayed the start of the barn by two weeks, and we had to get it under roof by the end of the summer. So we made our one concession: we hired a crew of four men for one day to help put a quick finish to the foundation so that Mike could begin the framing. If we had it to do over again, we would hire one good man to work along with Mike. With the foundation done, we suddenly realized that the barn was no longer just a hole in the ground. It was going up!

When the mortar was good and hard, we brushed a coat of protective foundation coating on all surfaces of the blocks that would be underground. (Use an old broom!) We laid a 4-inch perforated drainage pipe on gravel along the outside of the east and north barn wall and the

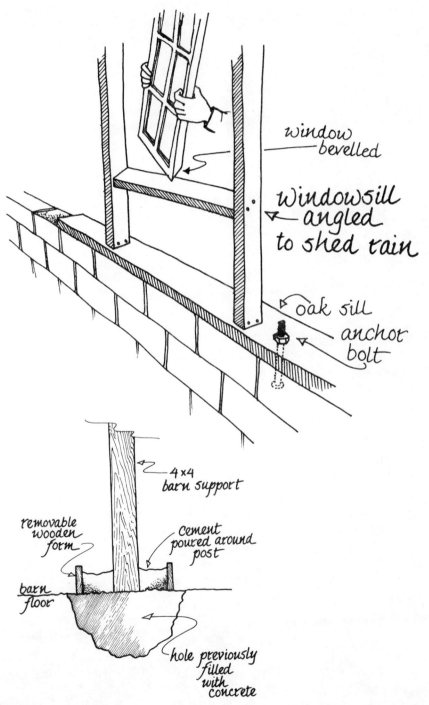

window
— bevelled

Windowsill
— angled
to shed rain

oak sill
anchor
bolt

4 x 4
barn support

removable
wooden
form

cement
poured around
post

barn
floor

hole previously
filled
with
concrete

low southwest corner. Then, when the tar foundation paint had dried, we hired a bulldozer to push the soil around the barn and fill in all the open spaces.

With the last (fourth) course of concrete blocks set in place, we called for the concrete truck again, this time to bring a soupy mix to fill in the spaces in the blocks. This is especially important at the corners. The concrete hardens into a pillar (inside the blocks) that supports the weight of the barn. We had enough concrete delivered to fill in most of the concrete block spaces.

While the concrete in the concrete blocks was still soft, we set anchor bolts at 3-to-4-foot intervals. These would be the connecting link between the hard, unyielding concrete foundation and the live wood that would frame up and fill out the barn. Mike drilled holes in 2-by-6-inch oak boards (the sill plates) to accept the protruding anchor bolts, two to a plate. The sill plates were then fastened in place by screwing the nut down on the bolt. Now we could nail the framing to them.

For studs we used 2 by 4s, toenailed to the sill plate every 24 inches on center, except at window spaces where they are set exactly far enough apart to allow a tight fit for the set-in windows, which are of several different sizes. We made the windowsills of 2 by 4s, set at an angle facing outward so that rain would run off rather than back down into the barn. We put the windows in later to avoid breakage. Studs were also nailed in place around the L-shaped interior wall where the pens would be, leaving spaces for gates.

The loft is supported by two interior 4-by-4 posts, toenailed to a 2-by-6 plate which is nailed to cement poured into a hole in the ground. (See diagram). A beam formed of two 2 by 10s connects the two 4-by-4 posts and supports the joists on which the loft planking rests. Two-by-6 joists are adequate; we used some 3 by 6s because we had them.

We braced all the corners with 2 by 4s. Bracing makes the structure rigid and able to withstand wind pressure. Everything we did, of course, checked with a good level. (The barn turned out to be truer to plumb than the house we live in!)

Once the first floor studs were up and braced, the next step was to nail on the plate that would support the second floor studs. We used 2 by 4s for the plate, cutting them so that when joined they met squarely in the center of the first floor stud, for stability. The plate was nailed to the studs all around.

South side:

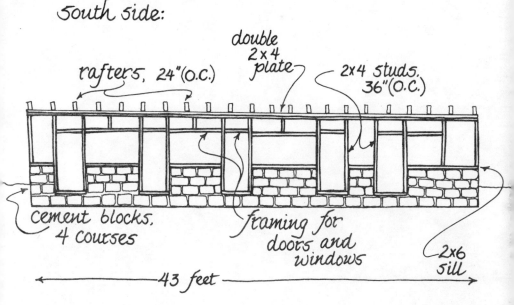

rafters, 24"(O.C.)

double
2 x 4
plate

2x4 studs.
36"(O.C.)

cement blocks,
4 courses

framing for
doors and
windows

2x6
sill

← 43 feet →

The second floor studs were then toenailed to the plate on the north and south sides of the barn, using the same spacing as on the first floor (24 inches O.C.). East and west side studs were cut later to fit the pitch of the roof.

For the north and south sides of the barn, we nailed a double plate of 2 by 4s to the studs, and braced the whole rack to the rigid first floor beam until it was securely fastened and the rest of the structure was complete.

We nailed oak planking to the joists to form a loft floor and brought ladders, tools and water jug up to the loft of the barn. The barn was slowly but surely being raised.

We needed the support of the loft floor in order to raise the roof. The ridgepole is supported by double 2 by 4s that are in turn stabilized by crossbracing. A 2 by 4 nailed to each side of the ridge gives additional support to the rafters. Once these supports were nailed in place, the ridgepole went on—a moment of great excitement. We tied a ribboned cedar bouquet to this highest point.

The next job, wrestling the rafters into place, brought us back to reality after the thrill of raising the ridgepole. The rafters were heavy

The rafters and furring strips are up.

Greg Bubel

Roofing the barn.   *Nancy Bubel*

The framed, roofed barn ready for siding.

Nancy Bubel

and the footing was sometimes precarious, but gradually the rafters fanned out—22 on the south side, then 22 on the north—each nailed to the ridgepole and the loft studs.

One more step remained before we could roof the barn—furring strips had to be nailed, 17 inches apart on center, across the rafters. The roof would then be nailed to these strips. The furring strips we used were about 1 by 2 inches and made mostly of oak, but that is just what we had. If we had bought new wood we would have used softwood. It helps to sew padded patches on your jeans' knees for the day you nail furring strips. There's just no place to get comfortable up there!

We used ridged aluminum roofing applied with special roofing nails, each supplied with a rubber washer to seal out rain. Cedar shingles would have been our first choice, but we hadn't the time to make them, and they were too expensive to buy. Mike had a day's help from each of two different friends when doing the roofing. He certainly needed someone up there to hold his feet while he lay face downward on the roof nailing the roofing at the edge where there was no toehold! The ridgecap went on last, overlapping the joint on the ridge between the north roof and the south, to keep rain and snow from blowing in on the loft.

Well, the roof was on. We heaved a sigh of relief and went on to the next thing—siding. There was just enough old tongue-and-groove barn siding to enclose our new barn. We measured and cut each

the ridgepole is up!

piece individually, a slow but sure process. Some that were warped or damaged on the surface we turned inside-out. When working with old wood, treat those tongues with respect. If too much tongue is broken the bond between the siding strips will be poor and rain will wash in and soften and rot the good wood. Mike found that he could persuade the old boards to fit together by tapping up and down their length with a hammer. The vibrations thus set up helped to join the tongue to the groove.

Since we had too few long siding pieces to complete the north side, we pieced what we had and made it do by applying siding first to the lower story between sill plate and first floor plate, then nailing a shorter course of the siding to the upper story between the first floor plate and the loft plate, slightly overlapping the lower course as shingles would overlap.

The door leading outside from the loft is made of the same tongue-and-groove siding, braced on the inside. The ventilators, two on the west side and two on the east, were on the old barn we had taken down. Mike shortened them to be more in scale with our building.

The windows are hung by hinges from 2 by 4s set between the studs. The doors are mostly salvaged and cut down from the used wood and findings we had bought. Several were made "new" from old tongue-and-groove. We used the old latches that were on the doors.

Side view:

double - 2x4 ridgepole supports

rafters

furring strips

ventilator framing

window framing

loft joists

2x4 studs, 24"(o.c.)

double 2x6 plate

cement blocks

2x6 sill

34 ft.

Fitting out the inside of the barn was done gradually as we moved our animals from their temporary quarters and acquired new animals. Partitions between the pens are made of old barn boards of varying widths nailed to 2 by 4s that in turn are nailed between the studs. The hens have furring strips nailed between 2 by 4s on two sides of their pen, with a furring strip door and wire fencing nailed to the pen side that faces on the interior of the barn. In four pens, mangers are built into the interior wall, between the studs. We make the manger sides good and deep (24 inches or so) to accommodate the weeds we cut for the goats in summer and to keep the goats from climbing out. The partition between the buck pen and the neighboring pen is 6 feet high and made of extra strong boards.

The barn is supplied with cold water and electricity. We used a secondhand sink, and ran an underground plastic pipe from the house to provide running water. (Mike left a gap in the concrete block barn foundation for the pipe.)

The sink drains through a 2-inch plastic pipe to a gravel bed some distance from the barn. No washing-up chemicals or detergents are used at the sink, only hand soap.

In the trench in which the water pipe is buried, we have an electric cable running from the house to the barn. A switch in the kitchen enables us to turn off all current to the barn.

There are many places in the barn that can't be shown on any diagram, where we added braces, nailed in cleats, reinforced a joint for good measure and otherwise made our own spur-of-the-moment response to a situation we had nailed ourselves into. These improvised bits of carpentry make the building strong, though. It is a building without pretense. Our mistakes and improvisations show. But it is sturdy, plumb, built to last, and pleasant to work in. We are pleased with it. Having used it through three years, we have discovered only one thing we want to change: The rammed-earth workshop floor is very dusty to work in. We've decided to surface it with cement.

We had visited several homemade barns before planning our own. Now, if you were to ask our advice on building *your* barn, I suppose we'd say something like the following:

1. Trust yourself. You know your animals, your plans for your herd, your own working habits. Don't be afraid to try your hand at designing plans or modifying existing plans.

2. Get a supply of graph paper and plan the whole building to scale, from all angles.

3. Make the best use of warmth from sun and shade from trees in choosing your building site.

4. Make use of sound used wood if you can, even if it necessitates modifying your plans.

5. Put your visitors to work.

6. Level everything you nail.

7. Work by the day. Building a barn is a big job, but like other big jobs it does get done when worked at steadily.

The newly completed barn.

Greg Bubel

Barn loft door ajar. Ventilators above the door were taken from an old barn and cut to scale for our structure.

This outside door to the hen pen, with its "customized" opening permitting the birds to hop out into their yard, is just an old brooder house door turned upside down; the present "hatch" door was the former window. We added a hinged board that hooks to the inside of the door and makes it possible to close the opening in bad weather.

Mike Bubel

Greg Bubel

Mike opening the hay loading door to the barn loft.

181

8. Use temporary braces to keep your structure plumb until the whole thing gets tied together by connecting walls, beams and studs.

9. It is easier to do it right than to do it over—an old folk saying we quote to each other. You can guess why.

For the record, we would have to say that the person who did all the designing, measuring, sawing, drilling, nailing and scaffolding acrobatics was Mike. He knew where the whole thing was headed, or seemed to. The ground-hugger who carted concrete blocks, helped check the level, chose boards, found the carpenter's pencils and steadied the teetering ladder was Nancy. Greg and Mary Grace, then 12 and 14, mixed mortar, steadied studs, pulled nails, nailed loft planking, and braved the loft catwalks and the roof. It took the four of us to do it. But now, heading for our barn to check on the new goat kids in the early morning light, each of us experiences that warmth of satisfaction that can only come from having participated.

MATERIALS LIST

1¼-inch nails—aluminum, for roof
ridge cap, aluminum
aluminum roofing (22 8-foot, 11 10-foot, and 11 sixteen-foot pieces).
furring strips
rafters—44 total
posts
beams
gate hardware
cement nails
roofing nails
16 anchor bolts
creosote
16,000 pound 2B stone
15 bags regular cement
foundation coating—10 gallons
2½ tons of sand
concrete for footings, mixed at site—5¾ yards of 1 by 2 by 4
concrete (transit mix)—2.5 tons poured into concrete block foundation

fencing
locust and cedar posts
windows
ventilators
planking
secondhand sink
electric cable—100 feet
plastic pipe—200 feet of ¾-inch plus coupling
100 feet of 1½-inch plus coupling
160 feet of 3-inch plus coupling
concrete blocks
door latches (old)
assorted common nails & spikes, plus cement-coated nails and special
spiral cement nails.
tongue-and-groove siding and flooring
2 x 4s
3 x 6s
2 x 10s
4 x 4s
1 x 2s and other assorted used lumber

You can plan it.
You can make it.
You can find the stuff to do it.
Go ahead!

The Woodbutcher's Bookshelf

Just in case you want to read more before you pick up your crowbar and hammer, here are some additional sources of information, directions and inspiration:

1. *The Owner-Builder and the Code: Politics of Building Your Home* by Ken Kern, Ted Kogon and Rob Thallon. Oakhurst, Ca.: Owner-Builder Publications, 1976.

2. *The Green Wood House: How to Build and Own a Beautiful, Inexpensive House.* by Larry M. Hackenburg. Charlottesville, Va.: U. of Virginia Press, 1976. On building with unseasoned wood.

3. *One Man's Forest: Pleasure and Profit from Your Own Woods* by Rockwell R. Stephens. Brattleboro, Vt.: Stephen Greene Press, 1974. Some good how-to's if you're cutting your own trees for lumber.

4. *Fences, Gates and Bridges: A Practical Manual* by George A. Martin. Brattleboro, Vt.: Stephen Greene Press, 1974. A reprint of a still-relevant 1887 book.

5. *Other Homes and Garbage: Designs for Self-Sufficient Living* by Jim Leckie, Gil Masters, Harry Whitehouse and Lily Young. San Francisco: Sierra Club Books, 1975. About alternative architecture, energy production, water supply and waste handling.

6. *Basic Construction Techniques for Houses and Small Buildings Simply Explained* by The Bureau of Naval Personnel.

7. *In Harmony With Nature: Creative Country Construction* by Christian Bruyere and Robert Inwood. New York: Drake, 1975. On log construction.

8. *Country Comforts* by Christian Bruyere and Robert Inwood. New York: Drake, 1975. More on homestead water systems, smoke-houses and such.

9. *How to Use Tools* by Alfred P. Morgan. New York: Arco, 1955.

10. *The Sensuous Gadgeteer* by Bill Abler. Philadelphia: Running Press, 1973. On using tools, improvising, working with materials.

11. *Practical Farm Buildings: A Text and Handbook* by James S. Boyd, Ph.D. Kansas City, Mo.: Interstate, 1973.

12. *Low-cost Pole Building Construction* by Doug Merrilees and Evelyn Loveday. Charlotte, Vt.: Garden Way, 1975.

13. *Craftsmen of Necessity* by Christopher Williams. New York: Random House, 1974. Open your mind to practical, imaginative building techniques developed by other cultures.

14. *Cloudburst One* and *Cloudburst Two: A Handbook of Rural Skills and Technology.* Berkeley, Ca.: 1973. (Two volumes)

Index

A

Aluminum, for roofing, 5, 63
Apron, carpenter's, 53

B

Barn, building of, 163-183
Bench grinder, 46-47
Body mechanics, in doing heavy work, 41-43
Bracing, 63
Building codes, 57
Buildings, pole, 62
    used, 9
        salvage of, 11-18

C

Cement blocks, 169-172
    foundations, 61
    woodpiles and, 20
Chisels, 52
Claw hammer. *See* Hammer, claw
Compost heap, plaster in, 9
Construction, 55-64
    appropriate materials, 57-60
    cutting, 65
    nailing, 65-69
    planning, 55-57
    screwing, 69-70
Copperheads, location of woodpile and, 20
Creep, small animal, 101-103
Crowbar, 28
Cutting, wood, 65

D

Drainage, 56-57, 61, 126
Drills, 49
Dumps, sources of salvage, 5

E

Exercise platform, for goats, 105-107

F

Feed bin, 141-144
Files, 49-52
Firewood, with nails, 28
Footings, 60
Foundations, 56, 60, 165

G

Garage, from logs, 75-81
Gates, 130-132, 139, 145-152
Goats, 101, 105, 115, 120

H

Hammer, claw, 48-49
    nail removal and, 27-28
Hay mangers, 115-120
Hay platform, for wood storage, 24
Hay rake, 95-98
Hinges, on gates, 147-151

L

Latches, 145-146
Levels, 49
Levering, 36-41
Logs, building with, 75-81, 153-161

M

Mallet, rubber, 52
Measuring tapes, 52
Moving, wood, 34-43, 78-79, 160

N

Nails, 59, 65-69
    removal of, 27-28, 30
    storage of, 28
    straightening of, 25
Newspaper plates, as shingles, 5

W

Walls, 62-63
Wood, green, 57-58
    used, 3-4
        cracks in, 59-60
        finding of, 8-9
        removing nails in, 27-28
        sources, 4-7
        storage, 19-24
Woodpile, 3, 20
    building of, 22-24
Wunderbar, 52
    for nail removal, 28